Historical American Biographies

# HENRY DAVID THOREAU

## Writer, Thinker, Naturalist

Pat McCarthy

**Enslow Publishers, Inc.**

| | |
|---|---|
| 40 Industrial Road | PO Box 38 |
| Box 398 | Aldershot |
| Berkeley Heights, NJ 07922 | Hants GU12 6BP |
| USA | UK |

http://www.enslow.com

*To my friend, Linda Rabius,*
*who is always there when I need her.*

Library of Congress Cataloging-in-Publication Data

McCarthy, Pat, 1940-
    Henry David Thoreau : writer, thinker, naturalist / Pat McCarthy.
        p. cm. — (Historical American biographies)
    Summary: Describes the life of nineteenth-century American writer,
philosopher, and naturalist, Henry David Thoreau.
    Includes bibliographical references (p. ) and index.
    ISBN 0-7660-1978-0
    1. Thoreau, Henry David, 1817-1862—Juvenile literature. 2. Authors,
American—19th century—Biography—Juvenile literature.
    3. Intellectuals—United States—Biography—Juvenile literature.
    4. Naturalists—United States—Biography—Juvenile literature.
    [1. Thoreau, Henry David, 1817-1862. 2. Authors, American.
    3. Naturalists.] I. Title. II. Series.
    PS3053 .M38    2003
    818'.309—dc21

                                                    2002012335

Printed in the United States of America

10 9 8 7 6 5 4 3 2 1

**To Our Readers:**
We have done our best to make sure all Internet Addresses in this book were
active and appropriate when we went to press. However, the author and the publisher have no control over and assume no liability for the material available on
those Internet sites or on other Web sites they may link to. Any comments or sug-
gestions can be sent by e-mail to comments@enslow.com or to the address on the
back cover.

**Illustration Credits:** Courtesy Library of Congress, Brady-Handy
Collection, reproduced from the *Dictionary of American Portraits*, pub-
lished by Dover Publications, Inc., in 1967, p. 94; Courtesy National
Archives, Brady Collection, reproduced from the *Dictionary of
American Portraits*, published by Dover Publications, Inc., in 1967,
p. 49; From the Archives of the Thoreau Society and the Walter Harding
Collection, used with permission of the Thoreau Society, Lincoln, Mass.,
and the Thoreau Institute at Walden Woods: www.walden.org, pp. 10,
29, 33, 41, 65, 69, 77, 84, 87, 97; Enslow Publishers, Inc., p. 15; Pat
McCarthy, pp. 46, 58, 60, 62, 113; Reproduced from the Collections of
the Library of Congress, p. 101; Reproduced from the *Dictionary of
American Portraits*, published by Dover Publications, Inc., in 1967, p. 4.

**Cover Illustration:** Pat McCarthy (background); Reproduced from the
*Dictionary of American Portraits*, published by Dover Publications, Inc.,
in 1967 (Thoreau Portrait).

# CONTENTS

*Henry David Thoreau*

# 1

# A NIGHT IN JAIL

One warm evening in July 1847, Henry David Thoreau left his cabin at Walden Pond and walked two miles into the village of Concord, Massachusetts. Thoreau enjoyed the familiar walk through the countryside on his way to pick up a shoe he was having repaired.

But an unpleasant surprise awaited him when he reached the village. Constable Sam Staples stopped Thoreau and reminded him that he had not paid his poll tax for several years. (A poll tax is a tax on people of a community where each person is taxed the same, whether they are rich or poor.)

## Protesting Government Actions

Thoreau told Staples he was withholding the tax because he did not agree with some of the government's actions. He later wrote that he did not want to trace the course of his dollar "till it buys a man or a musket to shoot one with."[1] He was referring to government support of slavery and the Mexican War. The war had started as a border dispute, but many thought it was just a way to gain more land. Thoreau believed the United States had no business fighting the Mexicans. Also, he hated slavery, since he thought all people should be free.

Staples told Thoreau he would have to put him in jail until the tax was paid. Thoreau refused to pay, so he was locked inside the local prison.

## Thoreau's Jail Experience

Thoreau later wrote about his experience in prison,

> I did not for a moment feel confined, . . . It was like traveling into a far country, such as I had never expected to behold, to lie there for one night. It seemed to me that I never had heard the town-clock strike before, not the evening sounds of the village; for we slept with the windows open.[2]

After Staples locked Thoreau in the cell, the constable went home, took off his boots, and made himself comfortable. Soon a woman with a shawl over her head knocked on his door. His daughter Ellen answered, and the visitor paid all the poll taxes that Thoreau owed. Some historians believe the woman was Thoreau's Aunt Maria, his father's sister. Staples did not want to put his boots back on, so he waited until morning to release his prisoner. Staples later said his prisoner was "mad as the devil" at being released against his will.[3]

"In the morning," said Thoreau,

> our breakfasts were put through the hole in the door, in small oblong-square tin pans, made to fit, and holding a pint of chocolate, with brown bread, and an iron spoon. When they called for the vessels again, I was green [inexperienced] enough to return what bread I had left; but my comrade seized it, and said that I should lay that up for lunch or dinner.[4]

Thoreau said that once out of jail, he picked up his repaired shoe. He then joined a group of people with horses who were on their way to pick huckleberries. Only a half hour later, he found himself two miles away from his former cell and out amongst nature again.[5]

## Proving His Point

An old story says Thoreau's friend, poet and philosopher Ralph Waldo Emerson, came to visit him in jail. He asked, "Henry, why are you here?" Thoreau replied, "Waldo, why are you *not* here?" He meant that Emerson should be protesting unjust government actions, too. There is no truth to the tale, but it does show that Thoreau went to jail to prove a point.[6]

Local reaction was mixed. Emerson disapproved of the protest. He told Thoreau's friend, antislavery advocate Bronson Alcott, that the act was "mean and skulking, and in bad taste."[7]

Emerson wrote in his own journal, "My friend Mr. Thoreau has gone to jail rather than pay his tax. On him they [the government] could not calculate."[8] He meant the government expected that Thoreau would pay the tax, even though he disagreed with the government's actions.

Thoreau later used his stay in jail as a basis for a lecture and an essay entitled "Civil Disobedience." He justified his act as a protest against both slavery and the Mexican War:

> When a sixth of the population of a nation which has undertaken to be the refuge of liberty are slaves, and a whole country is unjustly overrun and conquered by a foreign army, and subjected to military law, I think that it is not too soon for honest men to rebel and revolutionize.[9]

Jailing Thoreau was actually illegal. Staples had the right to seize his property, but not to put him in jail.[10] The records show that in 1849, two years after he was sent to jail, Thoreau paid his $1.50 poll tax. He had made his point that concerned citizens should protest government actions they think are unfair.[11]

# 2

# GROWING UP IN CONCORD

On July 12, 1817, a boy was born to John and Cynthia Dunbar Thoreau in a farmhouse in Concord, Massachusetts. John worked for his mother, Mary Minott, on the farm that had belonged to her late husband, Jonas Minott. Boston minister William Ellery Channing, later a friend of Henry David Thoreau's, described the house:

> It was a perfect piece of our old New England style of building, with its gray, unpainted boards, its grassy, unfenced door-yard. The house is somewhat isolate and remote from thoroughfares; on the Virginia road, an old-fashioned, winding, at length deserted pathway, the more smiling for its forked orchards, tumbling walls, and mossy banks.[1]

John and Cynthia named the baby David Henry Thoreau. Twenty years later, the young man reversed

*Henry David Thoreau was born in this farmhouse in Concord, Massachusetts on July 12, 1817.*

the order of his first two names, becoming Henry David Thoreau. He had always been called Henry.

## Family Background

John Thoreau's grandfather, Philippe, and his wife, Marie, had come from France to Boston two generations before. Their son, John, married a Scottish girl, Jane Burns.

Cynthia Thoreau was the daughter of a minister, Asa Dunbar, and his wife, Mary Jones Dunbar. This side of the family was also Scottish.

Henry joined two older children, Helen, who was five, and John, two. Another sister, Sophia, was born in 1819.

## Henry's Hometown

Concord at the time Henry was growing up was a village of about two thousand people. White houses lined the tree-shaded streets, and shops bordered the village square. Nearby were low hills, swamps, forests, and ponds. The Assabet and Sudbury rivers met to form the Concord River.

The climate varied, from intense heat in summer to cold, snowy weather in winter. Fogs often rolled in from the sea. Henry called the days with a brisk west wind "washing days," as clothes hung on a line would dry quickly.[2]

The Thoreaus moved around a good bit during the first few years of Henry's life. When he was about a year old, they moved to the village of Chelmsford, Massachusetts. Here, according to Henry, "Father kept shop and painted signs." He had other memories of Chelmsford. "The cow came into the entry after pumpkins," he recalled. "I cut my toe and was knocked over by a hen with chickens."[3]

He learned that he would eventually die and, according to his religion, go to heaven. One day he came in from sledding and said he did not want to die and go to heaven, because he would not be able to take his sled to such a fine place.

Henry's mother told another story from his childhood. John and Henry slept together in the trundle bed, a small bed that could be stored under the big bed. John always went right to sleep, but Henry often lay awake a long time. His mother asked, "Why, Henry dear, why don't you go to sleep?"

"Mother," he said, "I have been looking through the stars to see if I couldn't see God behind them."[4]

From Chelmsford, the family moved to Boston, where Henry started school and his father taught. On Henry's fifth birthday, the children visited their grandmother. She took Henry, Helen, and John to Walden Pond, near Concord. Henry was excited over the water and the booming of the bullfrogs. When they left, he said he would like to live there.[5]

## Family Life at the Thoreau House

John and Cynthia got along well and made a pleasant home for their children. Cynthia was the dominant influence in the home. A lively, bustling woman, she rented the extra rooms out to boarders to add to the family income. The large, attractive, dark-haired woman was known for her love of talking.[6] She was cheerful and kind, and most people liked her. She provided nourishing, tasty food on a limited budget.

Cynthia Thoreau had strong opinions and was active in civic affairs. She belonged to the Concord Female Charitable Society and the Bible Society and was one of the founders of the Concord Women's Anti-Slavery Society. Cynthia Thoreau sometimes shocked society leaders with her outspokenness and the bright yellow ribbons on her hat.

John Thoreau, by contrast, was a gentle, quiet man who did not succeed at his early business endeavors. He was short and prematurely bald, with kind eyes and the large nose that all the Thoreaus had.[7] He loved to read and to play the flute.

The Thoreaus moved back to Concord when Henry was six. There, Henry's father finally found a business where he could be successful. He began making pencils and did quite well at it.

Both parents took the children on nature walks along the river and in the woods. This was the beginning of Henry's lifelong interest in nature.

## The Thoreau Children

Henry's sister Helen was intelligent and scholarly. Later when Henry was in college and she was teaching, he wrote letters to her in Latin.

Henry idolized his brother, John, who was charming, social, and very religious. His sense of humor and sunny nature made him many friends. John was an amateur naturalist and made a list of Concord birds that Henry used in his own study of birds.

Sophia, the youngest of Henry's siblings, was homely and awkward, but lively.[8] She loved flowers and painting and was devoted to Henry.

## Uncle Charles

The household also included boarders and assorted aunts and uncles who came and went. Most memorable was Uncle Charles Dunbar, Cynthia's brother. He was funny and knew all kinds of tricks. When he carted logs to Barrett's Mill, he sometimes leaped over the pair of oxen, then back again.[9]

Henry later wrote about Uncle Charles in his journal, saying, "Edmund Hosmer remembers [Uncle Charles's] tricks in the bar-room, shuffling cards, etc.; he could do anything with cards, yet he did not gamble. He would toss up his hat, twirling it over and over, and catch it on his head invariably."[10]

## School Days

When the Thoreaus moved back to Concord, Henry went to Phoebe Wheeler's infant school. Then he attended the public grammar school, a typical one-room schoolhouse with boys and girls of all ages. When he was eleven, his parents enrolled both him and John in the Concord Academy, which prepared boys for Harvard University and girls for teaching. The teacher, Phineas Allen, taught Greek and Latin, which Henry enjoyed.

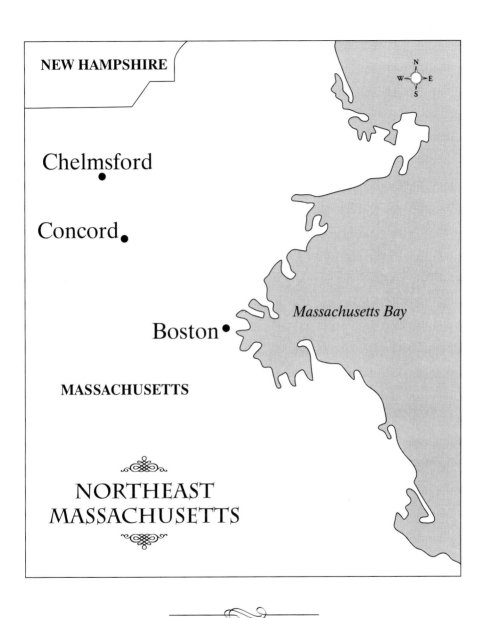

NEW HAMPSHIRE

Chelmsford

Concord

Boston

MASSACHUSETTS

Massachusetts Bay

NORTHEAST
MASSACHUSETTS

*The Thoreau family lived briefly in Chelmsford and Boston. (Thoreau would later attend Harvard in Boston.) However, Henry Thoreau would live most of his life in Concord. Walden Pond was just a few miles from the town center of Concord.*

Henry was a good student, but quiet. He was so serious that he was nicknamed Judge.

Although he did well in school, he did not mind missing it. He later recalled, "I remember how glad I was when I was kept from school a half a day to pick huckleberries on a neighboring hill all by myself to make a pudding for the family dinner. Ah, they got nothing but the pudding, but I got invaluable experience beside!"[11]

## Boyhood Activities

Henry participated in the normal childhood activities of the day. He drove the cows to pasture, ran barefooted through the grass, fished in the creeks, and hunted a little. Henry and his brother fished at night sometimes, using a spear. Their light was a fire in a tin pan with holes in the bottom, which they hung on the front of their boat. They made the spear by splicing a boar's tusk to a pole. Henry soon gave up hunting and fishing for the most part though, because he did not like killing.

Looking back on his boyhood, Henry wrote in his journal, "My life was ecstasy. In youth, before I lost any of my senses, I can remember that I was all alive, and inhabited my body with inexpressible satisfaction; both its weariness and its refreshment were sweet to me."[12]

With his brother, Henry roamed the fields and woods. He began early to look up the names of plants in a handbook. In the summer, the brothers swam. In the winter, they enjoyed ice-skating and sleigh rides.

During his boyhood, Henry, like his father, learned to play the flute, which he enjoyed the rest of his life.

The Concord Lyceum, an organization that presented public lectures, was a big part of Henry's life. It was established when he was twelve. The whole family attended the lectures, then discussed them.

At sixteen, Henry was ready to enter Harvard. The family had saved in order to send him. They had not been able to afford to send John, but now the pencil business was doing well. Also, Helen was teaching and could help with the fees.

## 3

# THE HARVARD YEARS

I n 1833, Henry Thoreau was off to college at the age of sixteen. Although he was young by today's standards, he was older than some college freshmen of the time.

His friend William Ellery Channing explained that just before Henry left, he asked his mother what profession he should choose. She replied, "You can buckle on your knapsack and roam abroad to seek your fortune." Channing said Henry was so distressed at the thought of leaving home that tears rolled down his cheeks. His sister Helen immediately put her arm around him and said, "No, Henry, you shall not go; you shall stay at home and live with us."[1]

## College Life

Life at Harvard then was quite different from college life today. It cost about $180 a year to attend. Henry did well enough to receive a twenty-five-dollar scholarship each year.

Biographer Robert D. Richardson says the Three *R*s at Harvard were rote learning (memorization without understanding), regimentation (strict routine), and rowdyism.[2] Rules were strict. The boys got up before sunrise in winter and attended church services in the bitterly cold chapel before breakfast. Thoreau wore his green homemade coat since he did not have the required black one.

Everyone ate in the commons, where they got three meals a day for $1.35 a week. Breakfast was hot coffee, hot rolls, and butter. The evening meal was just tea and cold rolls without butter. The noon meal was the only one that included meat. Sometimes the students would use their forks to attach a piece of meat to the underside of the table so they could have some meat with their supper.[3]

Despite strict rules, food fights at meals were frequent, and so was destruction of property. Thoreau's freshman year saw the most violent rebellion in the history of Harvard. Students rebelled against the rules, teaching methods, and the grading system. After a student riot, the entire sophomore class was expelled. Thoreau did not participate, but he agreed with many of the criticisms of Harvard.

There were 432 students when Thoreau started at Harvard, and a faculty of 25. A few buildings made up the campus, the streets were unpaved, and there were pigs in sties behind University Hall.[4]

Henry Thoreau shared room 20 in Hollis Hall with Charles Stearns Wheeler, who was from nearby Lincoln, Massachusetts. Thoreau's studies consisted of reading the classics, mathematics, a little science, and rhetoric (English composition). Thoreau also studied languages and left Harvard being able to read Greek, Latin, French, Italian, Spanish, and German.

Rhetoric teacher Edward Tyrrell Channing saw little promise in Thoreau, because Channing taught a different style than Thoreau was used to writing in. Actually, it took Thoreau years to get away from the formal style of writing Channing taught. Thoreau's later writing is much less formal and many people think it is more interesting to read.

The Harvard library opened a whole new world to Thoreau, and he spent hours there each day. He read all the classics and much literature of the day. He continued to borrow books from the library all his life.

His grades were high enough for him to receive the twenty-five-dollar scholarship each year and be asked to speak at commencement, the ceremony where graduates receive their diplomas.

Thoreau did not neglect his nature study while at Harvard. He often wandered along the banks of the Charles River. There he found the home of an ermine, a furry white animal, in the hollow of an apple tree. He visited it nearly every day that winter.

**Thoreau at Harvard**

This description of how Henry David Thoreau looked at Harvard was written by former classmate Reverend John Weiss after Thoreau's death:

> He passed for nothing, it is suspected, with most of us; for he was hard and unimpressible . . . How the prominent, gray-blue eyes seemed to rove down the path, just in advance of his feet, as his grave Indian stride carried him down to University Hall! . . . He did not care for people; his classmates seemed very remote. This reverie hung always about him, and not so loosely as the odd garments which the pious household care furnished. Thought had not yet awakened his countenance; it was serene, but rather dull, rather plodding. The lips were not yet firm; there was almost a look of smug satisfaction lurking around their corners . . . the nose was prominent, but its curve fell forward without firmness over the upper lip . . . Yet his eyes were sometimes searching, as if he had dropped or expected to find, something. It was the look of Nature's own child learning to detect her wayside secrets.[5]

## Thoreau Is Introduced to New Ideas

As was the custom at the time, Thoreau was excused to teach for a term. In December 1835, he went to Canton, Massachusetts, south of Boston, where he taught a class of seventy pupils for six weeks.

He was interviewed by the Reverend Orestes A. Brownson, and the two became fast friends. He boarded with Brownson, and the first night they sat up until midnight, deep in discussion. While Thoreau was there, they studied German together and discussed philosophy, religion, literature, and reform. Brownson, a Unitarian minister, was interested in reform and social change, and some of his enthusiasm rubbed off on Thoreau.

## Transcendentalism

The philosophy of transcendentalism began among the Unitarians in New England in the early 1800s. The movement was partly a reaction against strict Puritan attitudes. (The Puritans were one of the first Christian groups to live in New England.) Transcendentalism also opposed the strict rituals and narrow-minded beliefs of other established religions. Transcendentalists saw a direct connection between the universe and the person's soul. They had semireligious feelings toward nature. They thought people could become aware of truth through being aware of the natural world surrounding them. Most of the leaders of the movement were well-educated people who were writers.

A few years later, Thoreau wrote to Brownson, saying, "I have never ceased to look back with interest, not to say satisfaction, upon the short six weeks which I passed with you. They were an era in my life—the morning of a new Lebenstag [life]."[6]

## Thoreau Becomes Ill

During spring and summer 1836, Thoreau was ill and took time off from school. He wrote his friend Charles Wyatt Rice that summer, telling him the doctor had forbidden him to enjoy his favorite pastime—hunting for American Indian relics. For him that summer, "digging and chopping" for the relics was not allowed.[7] This illness was his first bout with the lung problems most of his family experienced. (Several members of the family died of tuberculosis, an infectious disease of the lungs.) He was able to return to Harvard in the fall.

## A Book Influences Thoreau

In spring 1837, Thoreau discovered *Nature* by Ralph Waldo Emerson. This small book had a tremendous impact on the young man. It reinforced many of his beliefs.

He related to passages like the following: "The lover of nature is he whose inward and outward senses are still truly adjusted to each other."[8] Thoreau bought a copy of the book for himself, and gave one to a classmate the next year.

*Nature* was a celebration of the wild, but it also introduced to the public the idea of transcendentalism. Transcendentalists believed that true religion could be experienced in nature, if a person were willing to open up to it. Henry David Thoreau, who had always been more at home in nature than in society, was fascinated by these ideas and began reading the work of the other transcendentalists.

A number of students high in the class ranking were asked to speak at commencement on August 16, 1837. Henry David Thoreau was among them. His topic was "The Commercial Spirit of Modern Times."[9]

He thought that the spirit of working, buying, and selling was good because it was a by-product of freedom, but bad because it was motivated by a love of wealth. He believed most of a person's time should be spent enjoying nature, rather than working.

Ralph Waldo Emerson gave the commencement address on "The American Scholar." Although Thoreau attended the ceremony, he did not pay five dollars for his diploma, saying, "Let every sheep keep

In his commencement address "The Commercial Spirit of Modern Times" Henry David Thoreau says that people should spend only one day a week working and the other six relaxing and enjoying nature:

*Let men, true to their natures, cultivate the moral affections, lead manly and independent lives; let them make riches the means and not the end of existence, and we shall hear no more of the commercial spirit . . .This curious world which we inhabit is more wonderful that it is convenient; more beautiful than it is useful—it is more to be admired and enjoyed than used. The order of things should be somewhat reversed,–the seventh should be man's day of toil, wherein to earn his living by the sweat of his brow, and the other six his sabbath of the affections and the soul, in which to range this wide-spread garden, and drink in the soft influences and sublime revelations of "Nature."*[10]

but its own skin, I say."[11] (At the time, diplomas were written on parchment made from sheepskin.)

## What Thoreau Learned at Harvard

Thoreau had a poor opinion of the quality of education he received at Harvard. When Emerson observed that Harvard taught all the branches of learning, Thoreau remarked, "Yes, indeed, all the branches and none of the roots."[12] He later wrote to Richard Fuller, brother of his friend Margaret who was editor of the transcendentalist magazine *The Dial*: "What I was learning in college was chiefly, I think, to express myself."[13]

Henry Canby, a Thoreau biographer, observes that at Harvard, Thoreau "was disciplined in the exactness, the accuracy, and the care for meaning which is the essence of scholarship."[14] This enabled Thoreau to carry on many studies of his own at Walden Pond and other places around Concord.

He also learned how to use the library, which was important to him the rest of his life. So although he was critical of his college education, he learned some valuable lessons. He was now ready to look at the future.

# 4

# THOREAU'S TEACHING CAREER

After college, Henry David Thoreau returned home. He was of medium height with sloping shoulders, and he walked with unusual energy. He had a pleasant, open face, with a flexible mouth, large nose, and strong, serious blue eyes, large and deep-set. When he walked, his eyes rarely left the ground.[1]

Thoreau was more independent in his thinking now and had some unconventional opinions. He wanted to live life as he wished, with plenty of freedom and time to think. Most men assumed they would have a job where they worked all day, but he cared only about making enough money to live. He secretly wanted to be a poet, but he looked for a job as a teacher.

Meanwhile, he helped his father with the pencil business. The country was in the midst of the worst depression (economic downturn) so far in its history, but he did not have to wait long to find a job.

## A Short-Lived Teaching Job

Thoreau was offered a good job teaching in the public elementary school in Concord, starting in September 1837. He would make five hundred dollars a year, which was very good pay at the time.

Thoreau had his own ideas about teaching, and they did not impress the members of the school committee. The first day of school he announced that there would be no physical punishment. The news quickly spread, and most adults thought that this was a crazy notion. They did not think he could control the students without beating them.

Two weeks after school started, Nehemiah Ball, a member of the school committee, came into the classroom. He told Thoreau that he must hit the disruptive students "or the school would spoil."[2]

Angry at being told how to teach, Thoreau called out six names at random. The children lined up, and he rapped each one on the knuckles with a ruler. None had misbehaved. He was showing that it did not matter whom he rapped on the knuckles, since he felt that physical punishment did not improve student behavior.

That evening, Thoreau resigned his job. He applied for positions in Maine, Kentucky, and Virginia, but the country's depression made it very difficult to find a job.

## Thoreau Meets Emerson

Thoreau went back to helping his father with the pencil business. This was when he met Ralph Waldo Emerson. Lucy Jackson Brown, sister of Emerson's wife, Lidian Jackson, was discussing one of Emerson's recent lectures with Helen Thoreau. Helen informed her that her brother, Henry, had written about similar ideas.

Helen showed Henry's writings to Brown. When Brown told Emerson about the incident, he wanted to meet Henry. They quickly became close friends. Emerson, at thirty-four, was fourteen years older than Thoreau, but he accepted him as a contemporary and equal.

Thoreau did not leave any record of their meeting, but Emerson wrote in his journal, "I delight much in my young friend, who seems to have as free and erect a mind as any I have ever met."[3] Later that month, he wrote: "My good Henry Thoreau made this else solitary afternoon sunny with his simplicity and clear perception . . . Everything that boy says makes merry with society, though nothing could be graver than its meaning."[4] He later remembered him as a "strong, healthy youth, fresh from college."[5]

Emerson had moved to Concord three years before, after his first wife died. He had given up his job as a pastor and concentrated on writing. Emerson became an inspiration to young people of the time, encouraging them to express themselves, revolt against outdated beliefs, and challenge the way things

*After reading Henry David Thoreau's words, Ralph Waldo Emerson (pictured) wanted to meet the writer, who shared the transcendentalist view of the world. This is a steel engraving made at the time.*

were done.[6] Thoreau learned from him that he must shape his own life and pursue his own goals.

## Thoreau Starts His Journal

Emerson encouraged Thoreau to keep a journal. Henry made his first entry on October 22, 1837, writing that someone had asked him, "What are you doing now? Are you keeping a journal?" He added, "So I make my first entry." He also wrote, "I seek a garret . . . The spiders must not be disturbed, nor the floor swept. . . ."[7] He lived in the garret, or attic, of the house where his family lived. That gave him privacy and time alone.

Emerson had earlier written in his journal,

> If life were long enough, among my thousand and one works should be a book of nature . . . It should contain the natural history of the woods around my shifting camp for every month of the year . . . No bird, no bug, no bud, should be forgotten on his day and hour.[8]

Emerson never wrote that book, but Thoreau did much the same thing in his journal.

Thoreau's journals show a passionate joy with the natural world. In the autumn of 1837 he wrote of his interest in the woods and fields, the river, his need for solitude, and the idea of living a primitive life. These early journals contained most of the major themes he would use in his books.

He also wrote about books he was reading, often copying lines he liked. He wrote down ideas for essays he wanted to write later. All the material for his books came from his journals.

Inspired by poets he read, including Henry Wadsworth Longfellow, William Shakespeare, and John Milton, Thoreau began writing poetry. Once, he wrote a poem, wrapped it around a bunch of violets, and tossed it into Lucy Brown's window. Emerson praised Thoreau's early poetry, writing that it was "the purest strain, and the loftiest, I think, that has yet pealed from this unpoetic American forest."[9]

Thoreau carried a notebook and pencil with him on his walks, so he could jot down thoughts and impressions of what he saw in the woods and fields. He used a spyglass (telescope) to watch birds and animals, and he carried an old music book of his father's, in which he pressed flowers and other plants he gathered.

Soon after he met Emerson, Thoreau started attending discussions at his friend's house. An interesting group met to discuss life, freedom of thought, and transcendentalism. Thoreau agreed with most of their philosophy, although in later years his beliefs became more scientific. He believed the transcendental view that a close association with nature was a means to finding spiritual truth.

## Transcendentalist Friends

At Emerson's house, Thoreau met Margaret Fuller, a writer and feminist; Elizabeth Peabody, who ran a bookstore in Boston; and George Ripley, a minister who started an idealistic community of transcendentalists called Brook Farm. Thoreau also met Bronson Alcott, and they became close friends when Alcott moved to Concord the next year. Alcott's daughter, Louisa May, later wrote many books, including *Little Women*.

## Henry Thoreau Starts a School

In June 1838, Thoreau decided to start a private school in the Parkman house, where the family lived. He started in June, with four boys who boarded there. He may have also had students who were not boarders but attended the school during the day. His brother, John, agreed to help when he could leave his job in West Roxbury.

Henry wrote to John, saying, "I am in school from eight to twelve in the morning, and from two to four in the afternoon. After that I read a little Greek or English, or for variety, take a stroll through the fields."[10] He also took care of the garden at home.

John came home on August 1, and the two brothers took a vacation. Then they reopened the school, with twenty-five students and a waiting list. Among the students were Bronson Alcott's daughters, Louisa May, Anna, and Beth. If students could not afford to go to the school, they were allowed to go for free.

The school moved to the old Concord Academy building, since the depression had caused the academy to close. This school was quite different from most schools of the time. Henry wrote to his friend Reverend Orestes A. Brownson:

> I could make education a pleasant thing both to the teacher and the scholar. This discipline which we allow to be the end of life, should not be one thing in the schoolroom, and another in the street. We should

*Henry David Thoreau was very close to his brother John (pictured).*
*The two brothers started a school together.*

seek to be fellow-students with the pupil, and we should learn of, as well as with him, if we would be most helpful to him.[11]

John interviewed students before they were admitted, telling them that they must really want to learn and must promise to follow the rules. If a student broke a rule, there was no physical punishment. Instead, John talked to the student. He related better to the students than Henry. Students enjoyed going out into the woods and fields with Henry, though, since he knew so much about animals and American Indians.

Henry taught natural history, science, and languages, and John instructed the children in math and English. The brothers took turns giving a talk to start the day. Once a week, they took the students on a walk, a sail, or a swim. Once when they sailed down the river, Henry told them why he thought a certain spot on shore could have been an American Indian camping place. The next week, he impressed them by uncovering the remains of a fire pit on that very spot.

The school reached the height of its success in April 1841. Then John suddenly became ill and the brothers announced the school would be closed. That marked the end of an experiment in education, as well as the last time that Henry David Thoreau had a full-time job. The Thoreau brothers had proved that children could learn in an atmosphere free from fear of physical punishment.

# A TRIP ON THE RIVER

Henry and John Thoreau had built a boat in the spring of 1839 and Henry said it had cost them a week's labor. Henry Thoreau described it as being "in form like a fisherman's dory, fifteen feet long by three and a half in breadth at the widest part, painted green below, with a border of blue."[1] He named it *Musketaquid*, the American Indian name for the Concord River. They had fitted the boat with wheels so they could pull it on land around waterfalls.

On August 31, 1840, while their school was on vacation, Henry and John Thoreau set out on a trip on the Merrimack River to New Hampshire, where they would climb Mount Washington.

At dawn they loaded the boat with a tent, blankets, books, and buffalo skins for their beds. They had two sets of oars, two sailing masts, and several poles for pushing the boat along in shallow places. They took potatoes and melons from the garden for food on their trip.

## The First Day

The Thoreau brothers went along the Sudbury, the Assabet, then the Concord River, passing under the Old North Bridge where the minutemen had fought the British in one of the first battles of the Revolutionary War. Everything was calm that first day, and it was a peaceful trip to Billerica, seven miles upriver.

They camped on the shore that night. "Here we found huckleberries," Henry wrote, "still hanging upon the bushes, where they seemed to have slowly ripened for our especial use. Bread and sugar, and cocoa boiled in river water, made our repast [meal]."[2]

Henry talked about the muskrat that swam by the boat that evening:

> The musquash [muskrat] by the boat is taking toll of potatoes and melons. . . . His presumption kindles in me a brotherly feeling. Nevertheless, I get up to reconnoitre [check out the surroundings], and tread stealthily along the shore to make acquaintance with him. But on the riverside I can see only the stars reflected in the water, and now, by some ripple ruffling the disk of a star, I discover him.[3]

The brothers lay awake a long time listening to the night sounds. Some were sounds of civilization—alarm bells, church bells, dogs barking. Others were sounds of the wilderness—a fox and the muskrat near the tent.

## Four Days on the River

On Sunday, September 1, John and Henry rowed six miles through the Middlesex Canal, which connected the Concord River with the Merrimack. Since the Merrimack River was lower than the Concord, they had to go through a series of locks, which lowered the boat to the level of the Merrimack. Sam Hadley, the lockkeeper, was happy to bring them through the locks, down the twenty-seven feet to the river.

That night they camped at Tyngsborough under some oaks. They were kept awake for a long time by some rowdy laborers on the railroad.

On the morning of September 2, they bathed at a sandy place in the river, then lay under some trees to

**On the River**

In his journal, Thoreau describes how he and his brother took turns investigating the shore on Monday, September 2, 1840:

*Occasionally one of us would run along the shore for a change; examining the country and visiting the nearest farm-houses; while the other followed the windings of the river alone, with the view of meeting his companion at some distant point, and hearing the report of each other's adventures—how the farmer praised the coollness [sic] of his well, and his wife offered the stranger a draught of milk. . . .* [4]

talk and rest. In the evening, they camped under pine trees near Nashua.

Tuesday, September 3, brought an early-morning fog. However, Henry wrote, "before we had rowed many rods [A rod equals 5.5 yards.], the sun arose and the fog rapidly dispersed, leaving a slight steam only to curl along the surface of the water."[5] They camped at Coos Falls in the town of Bedford, New Hampshire. Before they went to bed, they chatted with some workers in the area.

Wednesday, September 4, was their last day on the river for a while. They rowed past wooded islands and open country. Nearing Hooksett, New Hampshire, they encountered a series of canal boats. Henry described them in his journal: "With their broad sails set, they moved slowly up the stream in the sluggish and fitful breeze, as if impelled by some mysterious counter-current, like antediluvian [prehistoric] birds; a grand motion, slow and steady."[6]

Henry and John used the locks at the falls of Amoskeag "surmounting [going up] the successive watery steps of this river's staircase in the midst of a crowd of villagers, jumping into the canal, to their amusement, to save our boat from upsetting, and consuming much river water in our service."[7]

That night they got a loaf of homemade bread from a farmhouse and camped at Hooksett.

## Excursions on Land

The next morning the Thoreau brothers left the boat and set off on foot in the rain. They walked to

Concord, New Hampshire, that night. On September 6, they took the stage to Plymouth, then walked to Thornton, both in New Hampshire.

On September 7, they went to Franconia Notch to see the "Old Man of the Mountain." This rock formation looks like a man's face. It was later made famous by Nathaniel Hawthorne's short story, "Great Stone Face," written in 1850. The next two days, they explored the area and rested.

On September 10, they both climbed Mount Washington, the highest peak in the White Mountains, at 6,228 feet high. Henry called it by its American Indian name, Mt. Agiocochook. His journal entry for that day reads simply, "Sept. 10th ascended the mountain and rode to Conway."[8] The journey on the rivers seems to have made more impression on him than the climbing of the mountain.

## Home Again

The brothers took the stagecoach back to their boat. On Friday, September 11, 1840, they started home. The wind was strong and they made the whole fifty miles in one day. It was an exciting, invigorating trip, which Henry never forgot.

# 6

# LOVE AND PUBLICATION

E arlier the same summer of the Thoreau brothers'
trip on the river, they had both fallen in love—
with the same girl. She was Ellen Sewall, niece of their
boarder, Prudence Ward. Ellen was the daughter of a
Unitarian minister in Scituate, a nearby town. Ellen
and her mother arrived in Concord by stagecoach to
visit Ellen's grandmother and her Aunt Prudence.

The Thoreaus had met Ellen's eleven-year-old
brother, Edmund, a few months before and Henry
liked him very much. In his journal he described him
as "a pure uncompromising spirit."[1] He wrote a poem
about the boy. But he was even more impressed with
Edmund's sister, Ellen.

*Ellen Sewell captured the interest of both Thoreau brothers.*

## Henry Meets the Love of His Life

Ellen was seventeen and very pretty, with a slightly upturned nose, delicate lips and chin, and soft, lovely hair.[2] The day she arrived, Henry wrote a poem in his journal, entitled "The Breeze's Invitation." One line said, "I the king and you the queen."[3] Five days later, he wrote, "There is no remedy for love but to love more."[4]

Both John and Henry showed her around town, took her walking and boating, and chatted with her on the lawn in the evening. Neither brother knew the other was in love with her. Henry had always been cautious, awkward, and shy with girls.

Soon after Ellen went home, John and Henry made their trip on the river. When they returned, John went to Scituate to see Ellen. Her parents were away, so they walked the beaches unchaperoned. She wrote to her Aunt Prudence, "You have no idea how much pleasure Mr. John's visit has afforded us."[5]

## Henry and John Visit the Sewalls

In December 1840, both brothers visited the Sewalls, taking Prudence Ward with them. Henry took Ellen's father a book of poems. He walked alone on the beach, composing the poem, "The Fisher's Son." Meanwhile, John and Ellen walked together and talked.

When the brothers got home, Henry sent Ellen poems he had written, and John sent opals, lovely milky stones, for her rock collection. She wrote to both of them that winter. In June 1841, she was back for another visit.

## Henry Entertains Ellen

Henry took Ellen rowing and wrote in his journal, "The other day I rowed in my boat a free, even lovely young lady, and as I plied [rowed] the oars, she sat in the stern [back end of a boat], and there was nothing but she between me and the sky."[6] He also took her to a party where phrenology (a system of analyzing character by the shape of the skull) was the theme. He felt the bumps on her head and made everyone laugh when he said she had none, which meant either genius or idiocy.[7] Today, most people no longer believe in phrenology.

## A Short Engagement

When Ellen returned home, John accompanied her. While he was at her home, he asked her to marry him. She accepted. Henry did not stand in his way. His family and friends all agreed that he sacrificed his own desires in this matter to those of his beloved older brother.

However, when Ellen broke the engagement a few weeks later, Henry wrote of a wave of happiness that "flows over me like moonshine over a field."[8] This showed his relief that she would not marry John. Ellen's parents had insisted she break the engagement. They thought the Thoreaus were too radical in their opinions, although John was more conventional than

Henry. The Sewalls sent Ellen to Watertown, New York, to visit her uncle for a while.

## Henry Is Disappointed

Now Henry decided to try his luck with Ellen, so he sent a letter of proposal to her in Watertown. Her answer was brief and unfeeling. She wrote her Aunt Prudence and said that her father had told her to write "a short, explicit, and cold reply." She said "I do feel sorry H. wrote to me . . . I never felt so badly at sending a letter in my life."[9]

Henry was disappointed and never forgot her, but he was resigned to losing her. He dreamed of her occasionally. Ellen later told her daughters that it was "a very beautiful letter" that he wrote proposing to her.[10]

Later she wrote in her diary, "I wonder if his thoughts ever wander back to those times when the hours sped so pleasantly and we were so happy. I think they do. I little thought then that he cared for me so much as subsequent events have proved."[11]

When he was dying, Henry confessed to his sister Sophia, "I have always loved her."[12]

In the summer of 1840, Henry first broke into print. *The Dial*, a magazine started by the transcendentalists, published his poem, "Sympathy," in their first issue in July. It was a poem about Edmund Sewall, Ellen's brother.

# 7

# WRITER,
# LECTURER, AND
# HANDYMAN

After John and Henry David Thoreau closed their school in March 1841, Henry thought of buying a farm, and even put a down payment on one. However, the owner's wife refused to sign the deed with only a ten-dollar down payment.

## Life With the Emersons

Ralph Waldo Emerson invited Thoreau to come live at his house in exchange for serving as handyman, companion, and babysitter. Thoreau moved in on April 26. Emerson traveled a lot on lecture tours. He knew Thoreau was reliable, and Lidian and the children liked him.

Thoreau worked in the garden, helping Emerson and Lidian, who was a good flower gardener. In the orchard, he planted trees and grafted fruit trees. (Grafting attaches limbs from one tree to another tree.) He was also good at fixing things. These were peaceful days, and he had lots of time to himself for his long walks and his writing.

Thoreau was more than a handyman to the Emersons. He was a good friend and became part of the family. He and Lidian became very close. When he moved in, the Emersons' son, Waldo, called Wallie, was almost five, and their daughter, Ellen, was two. That November, a third child, Edith, was born. Henry was very fond of little Wallie and spent hours talking to him as the little boy followed him around, "helping" Thoreau with his chores.

*Henry Thoreau became part of the family when he moved into the Emersons' house.*

## Thoreau Makes More Friends

During his time at Emerson's, Henry David Thoreau became closer to him and the other transcendentalists. He met Nathaniel Hawthorne, a novelist, who wrote *The Scarlet Letter*. Hawthorne liked Thoreau at once and admired his closeness with nature.

Hawthorne's daughter, Rose Hawthorne Lathrop, described an afternoon of ice-skating:

> One afternoon, Mr. Emerson and Mr. Thoreau went with him [Hawthorne] down the river. Henry Thoreau is an experienced skater, and was figuring . . . dances and . . . leaps on the ice—very remarkable, but

**Hawthorne's Opinion of Thoreau**

Nathaniel Hawthorne was an author and friend of Henry Thoreau's. He would go on to become world famous upon the publication of *The Scarlet Letter* in 1850. Here, Hawthorne gives his opinion of his friend:

> *Mr. Thoreau is a singular character; a young man with much of wild, original Nature still remaining in him . . . He is as ugly as sin; long-nosed, queer-mouthed, and with uncouth and somewhat rustic manners . . . But his ugliness is of an honest and agreeable fashion, and becomes him much better than beauty . . . he has repudiated all regular means of getting a living, and seems inclined to lead a sort of Indian life . . . He is a keen and delicate observer of Nature . . . a genuine observer, which I suspect is almost as rare a character as even an original poet. And Nature, in return for his love, seems to adopt him as her especial child; and shows him secrets which few others are allowed to witness.[1]*

very ugly, methought. Next him followed Mr. Hawthorne who, wrapped in his cloak, moved like a self-impelled Greek statue, stately and grave. Mr. Emerson closed the line, evidently too weary to hold himself erect, pitching head foremost, half lying on the air.[2]

Thoreau also became friendly with William Ellery Channing, a young Unitarian minister. They spent a lot of time walking, but Thoreau wrote in his journal that Channing was frequently a wearisome companion, full of overemphasis and exaggeration. Channing loved nature and had once lived alone in a log hut in the wilds of Illinois. He dreamed of being a poet but was not successful.

## Thoreau Becomes Restless

Thoreau enjoyed life at the Emersons', but at the same time he was restless and wanted to be independent. On Christmas Eve he wrote in his journal, "I want to go soon and live away by the Pond, where I shall hear only the wind whispering among the reeds."[3]

## Tragedy Strikes

On New Year's Day 1842, Thoreau's brother, John, cut his finger. A week later, tetanus (an infectious disease that causes the body to become rigid) set in. John complained of stiffening in his jaws, then suffered terrible spasms. Henry David Thoreau left the Emersons' and went home to help. A doctor was called from Boston but could do nothing. On January 11, after two days of suffering, John died in his brother's arms.

Nathaniel Hawthorne, another one of Thoreau's friends, became world-famous for his novel The Scarlet Letter. The novel is about a married woman who is outcast from a strict religious society after having an affair.

John's death was a horrible shock to Henry Thoreau—one he never totally recovered from. Soon he suffered the same symptoms his brother had, but he did not have tetanus. Sometimes a person will suffer the same symptoms as someone close to him has, without having the disease. This is called sympathetic pain. Thoreau recovered in a few days. He did not write in his journal for almost six weeks. He finally wrote, "I feel as if years had been crowded into the last month."[4]

## Loss of a Child

To make matters worse, Wallie Emerson came down with a sore throat and fever on January 22. He died six days later, from scarlet fever. Thoreau wrote to Lucy Brown, ". . . he died as the mist rises from the brook, which the sun will soon dart his rays through. Do not the flowers die every autumn? He had not even taken root here. I was not startled to hear that he was dead; it seemed the most natural thing that could happen."[5] He was saying that the child's death seemed a part of nature, as flowers bloom, then die at the end of summer.

## Writing at the Emersons'

Despite his grief, Thoreau accomplished a good deal of writing during his two-year stay with the Emersons. He spent most of October and December 1841 copying the entries from his two ragged journals into five new blank books.

Much of his work, both poetry and essays, appeared in *The Dial*, the transcendentalist magazine. Emerson had taken over as editor, and Thoreau helped with the editing. He enjoyed this a great deal, and editing the work of others taught him to edit his own writings.

In May, Thoreau wrote an essay he called "Natural History of Massachusetts." This was the beginning of his move toward becoming more of a naturalist (one who studies and interprets nature). Emerson did not care much for the essay, but Hawthorne admired it.

## A Trip to a Mountain

That summer, Thoreau went on a four-day walk to Wachusett Mountain with Richard Fuller. Wachusett, the closest mountain to Concord, was a little over two thousand feet high. Thoreau wrote an account of the expedition, and it was published in a magazine called the *Boston Miscellany*. It was the first of his many travel essays.

Two years with the Emersons seemed to be enough for both parties. Hawthorne wrote, "Mr. Emerson seems to have suffered some inconvenience from his experience of Mr. Thoreau as an inmate. It may well be that such a sturdy, uncompromising person is fitter to meet occasionally in the open air than as a permanent guest at table and fireside."[6]

Thoreau was also getting restless. He was anxious to make some money from his writing. Emerson thought he needed to broaden his horizons. He got him a position on Staten Island, in New York, tutoring his brother William's son. Emerson thought Thoreau would have a good chance to sell his writing to New York publishers.

## Thoreau Moves to New York

Thoreau accepted the position and arrived on Staten Island in May 1843. Emerson wrote in his journal, "And now goes our brave youth into the new home, the new connexion, the new city."[7]

The move was a disaster. Thoreau had less privacy here, and he did not enjoy this family as much as he had Ralph Waldo Emerson's family. Thoreau did not particularly like the boy, whose name was Haven.

Thoreau hated the city, which he described to Emerson as "A thousand times meaner than I could have imagined. It will be something to hate,—that's the advantage it will be to me . . . The pigs in the street are the most respectable part of the population."[8]

New York was not impressed by Henry David Thoreau, either. He managed to sell only two pieces of writing, both to *The Democratic Review*. He submitted his writing to six other magazines without any luck. He wrote to his mother, "My bait will not tempt the rats; they are too well fed."[9]

He did enjoy the ocean, however, writing, "Everything there is on a grand and generous scale—sea-weed, water, and sand."[10]

## New Friends

In New York, Thoreau also met some people he liked. He wrote of Henry James, Sr., a philosopher: "I know of no one so patient and determined to have the good of you. He is a refreshing forward-looking and forward-moving man, and he naturalized and humanized New York for me."[11] James was against slavery, so the two had something in common. Thoreau never thought it was right for one person to own another and had worked against slavery in many ways.

Horace Greeley, antislavery editor of the *New York Tribune*, became a lifelong friend. Thoreau thought he was "cheerfully in earnest—at his office of all work—a hearty New Hampshire boy as one would wish to meet."[12] Greeley would later help Thoreau market some of his writing.

Thoreau was homesick the whole time he was on Staten Island. He wrote to his mother, "Methinks I should be content to sit at the back door in Concord, under the poplar tree, henceforth forever."[13]

## Home to Concord

He was back home in Concord before Christmas, living with his parents and helping with the pencil business. Thoreau was restless, though. His writing career had stalled. *The Dial*, his main publisher, went out of business in April 1844. And he still wanted to be able to support himself.

## An Unfortunate Blaze

An incident that April made him quite unpopular in Concord. He and a former pupil, Edward Hoar, went camping at Fair Haven Pond. They built a fire to cook their fish. The fire got away from them, spreading rapidly through the dry grass and into the woods. They tried to beat it out but could not. Thoreau sent Hoar in the boat to spread the alarm, while he ran through the woods to warn farmers. He ran two miles without stopping before he found help. By then, he was so exhausted, he just sat down and watched the fire.

People in Concord remembered the fire for years. Three hundred acres of woods burned. Many thought it showed how shiftless Thoreau had become. They thought he should settle down to a full-time job.

## A New Home for the Thoreaus

That fall, Thoreau helped his father build a new house for the family west of the railroad tracks, in an area of Concord called Texas. This gave him experience in building a house. The Thoreaus had never owned a house before, so they were very pleased with it. Henry dug the cellar and built the stone foundation walls.

Thoreau had been elected curator of the Concord Lyceum when he returned from Staten Island. He was given $109 for expenses and managed to provide the hall, light, heat, and twenty-five lectures for only $100. Emerson, Greeley, and Thoreau himself were among the lecturers.

However, Thoreau wanted to get away where he could be alone and observe nature. He had dreamed for years of living alone by a pond. Again, Emerson provided the way.

In October, Emerson bought fourteen acres of land on the shore of Walden Pond. Most of the land in the area was used for farming, but Walden Pond was

### Thoreau's Account of the Forest Fire

Here, Thoreau deals with the guilt of being responsible for a forest fire. In the end, he resolves that the flames are running their natural course, and even sits down to enjoy the fire. Many of the citizens of Concord did not look upon Thoreau as favorably after they learned how he reacted to the fire:

> I sat down to observe the progress of the flames, which were rapidly approaching me, now about a mile distant. Presently I heard the sound of a distant bell giving the alarm, and I knew the town was on its way to the scene. Hitherto I had felt like a guilty person—nothing but shame and regret. But now I settled the matter with myself shortly. I said to myself: "Who are these men who are said to be the owners of these woods, and how am I related to them? I have set fire to the forest; but I have done no wrong there; and now it is as if the lightning had done it. These flames are but consuming their natural food" . . . So shortly I settled it with myself, and stood to watch the approaching flames. It was a glorious spectacle, and I was the only one there to enjoy it.[14]

surrounded by woods. Emerson understood that Thoreau needed to get away and live on his own in order to write. He agreed to let Thoreau build a cabin and live at Walden Pond. At last, Henry Thoreau's dream from his youth would be realized, and only time would tell what challenges his new environment would bring.

# 8

# AT WALDEN POND

On July 4, 1845, Henry Thoreau moved to Walden. He wrote, "My purpose in going to Walden Pond was not to live cheaply nor to live dearly there, but to transact some private business with the fewest obstacles."[1]

For several years Thoreau had wanted to be independent, but he could not afford a place of his own. Emerson's offer to let him build a cabin at Walden Pond was the perfect solution. It would not cost much to live there, so by doing odd jobs, he could make enough money to live on. He would still have time for his long walks and his writing. He had wanted to live at Walden Pond since he was five.

Thoreau was always trying to get closer to nature and to simplify his life. At Walden, he would be able

*Henry Thoreau first eyed Walden Pond when he was a young boy. As an adult, his dream of living there became a reality. Here is how Walden Pond looks today.*

to do both. He wrote, "I went to the woods because I wished to live deliberately, to front only the essential facts of life, and see if I could not learn what it had to teach, and not, when I came to die, discover that I had not lived."[2]

William Ellery Channing and another friend Charles Stearns Wheeler had tried living alone in a hut. Channing encouraged Thoreau to try it.

## Building the Cabin

Thoreau began preparing the site. The cabin would overlook the lake, nestled beneath the pine trees. In his own words: "Near the end of March, 1845, I borrowed an axe and went down to the woods by Walden Pond, nearest to where I intended to build my house, and began to cut down some tall arrowy white pines, still in their youth, for timber."[3]

Thoreau dug a cellar in the sandy soil to store his potatoes in. He used the pine trees to make the frame of the ten- by fifteen-foot cabin. He needed boards for siding the house, so he bought a shack from James Collins, an Irishman. Thoreau paid $4.25 for it and hired a horse and cart to bring the boards back. He carefully tore the shanty apart, saving all the nails.

Soon he was ready for a house raising. Several men in the community helped, including his farmer friend Edmund Hosmer, William Ellery Channing, Bronson Alcott, and George William Curtis, who later became a writer and editor. Thoreau built the foundation for his fireplace from two cartloads of stones he had carried up from the pond in his arms.

## Thoreau Moves In

He celebrated his personal independence by moving in on July 4, 1845, Independence Day. His cabin had cost exactly $28.12 1/2. During the summer and fall, he built the chimney, fireplace, and stone hearth and plastered the walls. He described his house this way: "I have thus a tight shingled and plastered house, ten feet wide by fifteen long, and eight-feet posts, with a garret and a closet, a large window on each side, two trap doors, one door at the end, and a brick fireplace opposite."[4]

*A replica of Thoreau's cabin shows how small it was. This goes along with Thoreau's belief that one does not need a lot of material things to live a happy life.*

The time spent at Walden was the high point of Thoreau's life. His health had never been better, and he was very happy. "Sometimes, when I compare myself with other men, methinks I am favored by the gods. They seem to whisper joy to me beyond my deserts."[5]

Each morning when the weather permitted, he bathed in the pond. Sometimes he worked in his bean field or hoed corn in his bare feet. He went for long walks in the afternoons, even in the coldest weather. After his beans and corn were harvested, he spent most mornings reading and writing. Sometimes, Thoreau just wanted to spend time with nature.

## Housekeeping Tasks

With as few worldly goods as Henry David Thoreau had, it was not hard to clean house:

> When my floor was dirty, I rose early, and setting all my furniture out of doors on the grass, bed and bedstead making one budget, dashed water on the floor, and sprinkled white sand from the pond on it, and then with a broom scrubbed it clean and white; and by the time the villagers had broken their fast the morning sun had dried my house sufficiently to allow me to move in again, and my meditations were almost uninterrupted. It was pleasant to see my whole household effects on the grass . . . It was worth the while to see the sun shine on these things, and hear the free wind blow on them.[6]

His household goods consisted of a bed, a three-legged table, a desk, three chairs, a mirror three inches in diameter, a pair of tongs, andirons to hold the logs in the fireplace, a kettle, a skillet, a frying pan, a dipper,

*This is what the inside of Thoreau's cabin may have looked like.*

a wash bowl, two knives and forks, three plates, one spoon, a cup, a jug for oil, a jug for molasses, and a lamp. There were also his books, pen and ink, and paper.[7]

## Thoreau Enjoys Free Time

Thoreau thoroughly enjoyed his free afternoons. There were all kinds of choices to be made: "Shall I go down this long hill in the rain to fish in the pond? I ask myself. And I say to myself: Yes, roam far, grasp life and conquer it, learn much and live. Your fetters [shackles] are knocked off; you are really free. Stay till late in the night; be unwise and daring."[8]

Until he finished the fireplace, Thoreau cooked outside. He baked hoecakes (cornmeal cakes) and bread. He made a kind of molasses from pumpkins or beets, but liked maple sap better as a sweetener. He decided he did not need salt. He ate meat only when he ate with family or friends. He did eat fish and lots of vegetables, as well as wild berries, grapes, chestnuts, and hickory nuts.

Most of all, Thoreau enjoyed the simplicity of his new life. He wrote about it in his journal.

**Thoreau's Writings on Simplifying Life**

In *Walden*, Thoreau stressed the importance of simplifying life. He says that all people should keep their responsibilities to a minimum so that they have time to enjoy life:

> *Simplicity, simplicity, simplicity! I say, let your affairs be as two or three, and not a hundred or a thousand; instead of a million, count half a dozen, and keep your accounts on your thumb-nail. In the midst of this chopping sea of civilized life, such are the clouds and storms and quicksands and thousand-and-one items to be allowed for, that a man has to live, if he would not founder and go to the bottom and not make his port at all, by dead reckoning, and he must be a great calculator indeed who succeeds. Simplify, simplify.[9]*

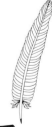

## Thoreau Was Not a Hermit

Although he lived by himself, Henry Thoreau certainly was not a hermit—one who lives completely apart from society—during his two years at Walden Pond. The pond was only two miles from Concord, and few days went by that he did not walk into the village to visit family or friends.

He enjoyed seeing people but was always happy to be back at Walden. He compared Concord to a prairie dog town. He said the village was "as curious to me as if they had been prairie-dogs, each sitting at the mouth of its burrow, or running over to a neighbor's to gossip."[10]

When Thoreau was in town late, he was ready to "launch myself into the night, especially if it was dark and tempestuous, and set sail from some bright village parlour or lecture room, with a bag of rye or Indian meal upon my shoulder, for my snug harbour in the woods."[11]

He had many visitors. He enjoyed talking with berry pickers who happened by, and he loved having children visit. He took the Alcott girls and other children for boat rides on the pond.

Channing and Alcott were frequent winter visitors, and the men had long discussions by the cozy fire in the little cabin. Thoreau sometimes read to Alcott from whatever piece of writing he was working on.

He liked Alek Therien, a French-Canadian woodchopper. Henry found him a "well of good humor and contentment which overflowed at his eyes."[12] The man loved his work, saying, "By George! I can enjoy

*May Alcott, daughter of Bronson Alcott and sister of Louisa May, drew this sketch of a man canoeing on Walden Pond. Her version of Thoreau's cabin can be seen in the background. Thoreau's cabin was not on top of a hill in real life.*

myself well enough here chopping; I want no better sport."[13]

Another friend was John Field, an Irishman living in a hut a mile or so away. Thoreau also entertained farmers, ministers, runaway slaves, fishermen and hunters, railroad workers, and a man from the poorhouse.

## Writing at Walden

Moving to the pond seemed to have released Thoreau's creativity, and he did a great deal of writing during his two years and two months at Walden. He wanted to write a book about his and John's trip on the rivers, so he went through his journals, numbering the paragraphs and putting them into the correct chapters. He started his first draft in the summer of 1845.

The book would be called *A Week on the Concord and Merrimack Rivers*. He condensed the two-week trip into one week and added other thoughts and essays from his journals.

He knew he would write about his stay in the woods, so he started two new notebooks. One is written in the present tense and the entries are dated. Into the other, he copied entries and edited them, adding other thoughts to them.

At Walden, he wrote two complete drafts of *A Week*, a complete draft of *Walden*, a lecture on his life in the woods, a lecture on author Thomas Carlyle, and the first third of his book, *The Maine Woods*. This is amazing, considering all the time he spent walking, observing nature, going into town, and entertaining company. Both his books that were published during his lifetime were written here.

## Thoreau as an Ecologist

Thoreau worried about the woods becoming less wild. He wrote, "When I consider that the nobler animals have been exterminated here—the cougar, the panther, lynx, wolverine, wolf, bear, moose, deer, the beaver, the turkey, etc., etc.—I cannot but feel as if I lived in a tamed, and, as it were, emasculated [weakened] country."[14]

He did not like farmers shooting hawks to protect their chickens, either. "I would rather never taste chickens' meat nor hens' eggs," he wrote, "than never to see a hawk sailing through the upper air again. This sight is worth incomparably more than a chicken soup or a boiled egg."[15]

## Thoreau Takes Thorough Notes

Thoreau took a great interest in documenting everything he saw—signs of the changes of seasons, behavior of animals, and even the ice on the pond, which he measured and tested at intervals. He watched the colors change in the pond—green in the deep places and blue in the shallow. Many birds—chickadees, wood thrushes, brown thrashers, and martins—entertained him with their songs. He watched a fish hawk dive for fish and listened to the loons' wild call. On summer evenings, he often heard an owl hooting.

Thoreau knew many people of Concord were not sympathetic to his experiment. "This was sheer idleness to my fellow-townsmen, no doubt; but if the birds and flowers had tried me by their standard, I should not have been found wanting."[16]

## Paying the Bills

Thoreau did do a certain amount of work at Walden and in the village to support himself. He cut down trees to clear the field, using the wood for firewood. He plowed the field and planted beans, corn, turnips, and potatoes.

His farming expenses were $14.72 1/2. His harvest included twelve bushels of beans, eighteen bushels of potatoes, and other vegetables. He made a profit of $8.72 1/2, and he figured that he ate $4.50 worth of his crops himself. He spent $8.74 for rice, molasses, rye, cornmeal, pork, sugar, lard, apples, dried apples, sweet potatoes, a pumpkin, and a watermelon.[17]

Thoreau proved to his own satisfaction that man does not need to spend most of his time earning money in order to support himself. He picked up a little extra money doing odd jobs in the village, but the majority of his time was spent in reading, writing, and enjoying nature. Of course, Emerson was allowing him to live on the land without cost.

## Thoreau as a Scientist

While at Walden, Thoreau became more interested in science. He found specimens of fish and other wildlife and shipped them to Louis Agassiz, a Swiss naturalist who had just come to America. Thoreau was able to provide specimens of two fish that Agassiz had never seen before.

## A Trip to Maine

During his second summer at Walden, in 1846, Thoreau traveled to Maine. He met his cousin, George Thatcher, in Bangor. They went by stagecoach to Mattawamkeag, which was as far as the road went. They poled a heavy wooden boat called a bateau up

*The Fitchburg Railroad ran near Thoreau's cabin at Walden Pond.*

the Penobscot River. After twenty-five miles, they entered North Twin Lake, which Thoreau considered the beginning of the real wilderness.

Their goal was Mt. Katahdin, which Thoreau called Ktaadn. At almost one mile high, it was Maine's tallest mountain, and Thoreau was determined to climb it. Thoreau climbed the mountain alone. He found the mountaintop to be a cold, harsh, windy place, totally primitive.

He concluded that "The tops of mountains are among the unfinished parts of the globe, whither it is a slight insult to the gods to climb and pry into their secrets."[18] He learned that not all of nature welcomes man.

Home again, he wrote about the trip, describing nature as an untamed place that made previous seasons of his life seem "unsubstantial and . . . incredible."[19] This would later become part of his book *Maine Woods*.

## Thoreau Leaves Walden Pond

By late summer 1846, Thoreau was ready to leave Walden Pond. He said he left the pond "for as good a reason as I went there. Perhaps it seemed to me that I had several more lives to live, and could not spend any more time for that one."[20]

He had accomplished his goals and decided to move on to other things. He wrote, "I learned this, at least, by my experiment; that if one advances confidently in the direction of his dreams, and endeavors to live the life which he has imagined, he will meet with a success unexpected in common hours."[21] He had proved he could actually simplify his life, not just talk about doing it.

Emerson was going on a lecture tour of Europe and asked Henry to stay at the house again and look out for Lidian and the children. So Thoreau left the cabin at Walden Pond on September 6, 1846, and moved back to the Emerson home.

# LECTURING AND TRAVEL

Would Henry Thoreau ever live at Walden Pond again? The answer is no, but he often missed the life he had led there. Four years later, in 1850, he wrote in his journal,

> But why have I changed? I left the woods? I do not think that I can tell. I have often wished myself back . . . Perhaps I wanted a change. There was a little stagnation, it may be . . . Perhaps if I had lived there much longer, I might have lived there forever. One would think twice before he accepted heaven on such terms.[1]

## Back With the Emersons

Although he sometimes missed Walden, Thoreau enjoyed life with the Emersons. Emerson sailed for England on October 5, 1846. Having lived there before, Thoreau was much at home with Lidian and the children. The Emersons now had another little boy, Edward, who was often called Eddy.

Thoreau wrote to Emerson in England:

> Lidian and I make very good housekeepers. She is a very dear sister to me. Ellen and Edith and Eddy and Aunty Brown keep up the tragedy and comedy and tragic-comedy of life as usual . . . He [Eddy] very seriously asked me, the other day, 'Mr. Thoreau, will you be my father?' I am occasionally Mr. Rough-and-tumble with him [he played with him] . . . So you must come back soon, or you will be superseded.[2]

## An Unwelcome Romantic Advance

Later on in the same letter, he wrote of a romantic problem he was having. "I have had a tragic correspondence," he wrote, "for the most part all on one side, with Miss F__. She really did wish to—I hesitate to write—marry me . . . I sent back as distinct a *no* as I have learned to pronounce after considerable practice."[3]

The original letter has been lost, and no one knows for sure who the lady was. Many think "Miss F__" was Margaret Fuller, who was in Europe at that time. She has been remembered as a member of the transcendentalist movement and editor of *The Dial*. The next year she married Angelo Ossoli, an Italian of noble birth.

Lidian was sick much of the time her husband was gone, and Thoreau helped her with guests.

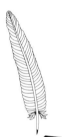

**Excerpt from Letter to Emerson**

In this letter to Ralph Waldo Emerson, Henry Thoreau relates Lidian's condition to her husband:

*Lidian is too unwell to write to you; so I must tell you what I can about the children and herself. I am afraid she has not told you how unwell she is, today perhaps we may say—has been. She has been confined to her chamber four or five weeks, and three or four weeks, at least to her bed—with the jaundice, accompanied with constant nausea, which makes life intolerable to her. . . . She is as yellow as saffron. The Doctor, who comes once a day does not let her read (nor can she now) nor hear much reading. She has written her letters to you till recently sitting up in bed—but he said that he would not come again if she did so.* [4]

## Thoreau Publishes Essays

Greeley had sold Thoreau's essay on Carlyle to *Graham's Magazine*, and it had been printed while he was still at Walden. However, it took Greeley until May 1848 to collect the seventy-five dollars due for it. He kept twenty-five dollars for expenses, and sent the other fifty dollars to Thoreau.

Greeley also sold the story about "Ktaadn" to *Union Magazine*, where it appeared in 1848. Besides the lectures, Thoreau worked a lot on *Walden* while at the Emersons'.

Ralph Waldo Emerson returned home in July 1848, and Thoreau went back home to live with his family. Helen was very ill with the family disease of tuberculosis.

## Thoreau's First Book

Also in 1848, Thoreau paid to have his first book, *A Week on the Concord and Merrimack Rivers*, printed. He signed the contract with Munroe & Co. and the proofs were printed before the end of the year. In May 1849, the thousand copies of the book were ready to sell.

Greeley got George Ripley to write a good review of the book in the *Tribune*. Poet and editor James Russell Lowell wrote about it for the *Massachusetts Quarterly Review*. Like many others, he liked the account of the journey, but he did not like the added material, feeling that Thoreau was preaching at people. Lowell did say, "The style is compact, and the language has an antique purity like wine grown colorless with age."[5]

Sophia Dobson Collet, a writer for the London *People's Review*, wrote glowingly of the book. She said, "The writer describes the scenery of his voyage with the vividness of a painter, and the scrutiny of a naturalist . . . The occasional digressions are . . . not unworthy to stand beside [the essays] of Emerson himself."[6]

Thoreau had borrowed money to pay for the printing, and he slowly paid it back from his proceeds from surveying and pencil making. The book was not very popular, selling only 219 copies.

## Family Reaction to *Walden*

By early 1849, *Walden* was nearly ready to be shown to a publisher. The whole family had read it, and they all told him what he should take out. Aunt Maria said in a letter,

> You know I have said, there were parts of it that sounded to me very much like blasphemy, and I did not believe they would publish it, on reading it to Helen the other day Sophia told me, she made the same remark, and coming from her, Henry was very much surprised, and said she did not understand it, but still I fear they will not persuade him to leave it out.[7]

However, as Thoreau completed one of his greatest accomplishments, tragedy struck. After a long illness, Helen Thoreau finally died of tuberculosis on May 2, 1849. While they were preparing to move the coffin to the cemetery after the service, Thoreau wound his favorite music box and let it play.

## Spending Time in Nature

Although he did not live at Walden anymore, Thoreau still lived for the time he spent enjoying nature. He spent hours on long walks, often with William Ellery Channing. "I cannot feel well in health and spirits without at least four hours a day sauntering through the woods and fields of Concord township; and longer than that if possible," Thoreau said.[8] He pitied the shopkeepers and mechanics, "who spend not only all the morning, but all the afternoon too [at their work.] . . . I think they deserve some credit for not having committed suicide long ago."[9]

Louis Agassiz, Thoreau's Swiss naturalist friend, came to Concord and hunted turtles and mice with Thoreau. In December 1849, a friend of Thoreau's shot a goshawk and he sent the body to Agassiz. After examining it, Agassiz determined that John James Audubon had been mistaken when he identified the goshawk as being part of the same family as the European falcon.

Thoreau earned most of his money by surveying. He had become very good at it. In the late 1840s, he bought an expensive set of instruments. He was well respected as a surveyor, and he liked the job because it did not have set hours.

## Spending Time With Channing

Thoreau had many friends during this time, but he spent more time with William Ellery Channing than with anyone else. They were good friends, but he described Channing as "naturally whimsical as a cow is brindled. He can be incredibly selfish and unexpectedly generous."[10] "Whimsical" means unpredictable;

*William Ellery Channing (pictured) knew Thoreau for most of his life. He even wrote a biography of Thoreau called* Thoreau: The Poet Naturalist.

**Channing's Description of Thoreau**

William Ellery Channing was a Unitarian from Boston and a good friend of Thoreau's. Channing gave a vivid physical description of his friend in his book *Thoreau: The Poet-Naturalist*, which was published in 1873:

> In height he was about the average; in his build spare, with limbs that were rather longer than usual, or of which he made a longer use. His features were marked; the nose aquiline or very Roman, like one of the portraits of Caesar (more like a beak, as was said); large overhanging brows above the deepest-set blue eyes that could be seen—blue in certain lights and in others gray; the forehead not unusually broad or high, full of concentrated energy and purpose; the mouth with prominent lips, pursed up with meaning and thought when silent, and giving out when open a stream of the most varied and unusual and instructive sayings. His whole figure had an active earnestness . . . his eyes bent on the ground, his long swinging gait, his hands perhaps clasped behind him, or held closely at his side—the fingers made into a fist.[11]

Thoreau is comparing Channing's unpredictable nature to the random pattern of a cow's markings. Channing had a sense of humor, which was important to the friendship.

## Other Good Friends

Harrison Blake, a man from Worcester, Massachusetts, wrote to congratulate Thoreau on an old article in *The Dial*, and their correspondence grew from there. They had attended Harvard at the same time but barely knew each other. Thoreau once wrote to Blake, "I am too easily contented with a slight and almost animal happiness. My happiness is a good deal like that of the woodchucks."[12] Blake became a great admirer of Thoreau.

Greeley was his most useful friend, acting as a sort of unofficial literary agent and selling his articles to magazines. Greeley wanted Thoreau to write about his prominent friends in Concord, including Emerson and Hawthorne. Thoreau refused to commercialize his friendships in this way.

## A Trip to Cape Cod

In the fall of 1849, Thoreau and Channing set off for Cape Cod. Thoreau called it "the bare and bended arm of Massachusetts."[13] He loved the Cape, with its bleak wind and driving rain and mist. He was fascinated by the desolate expanse of sand and sea. He watched in awe as the huge waves rolled in, roaring as they came. He felt that here at the end of the Cape, a man could put all America behind him.[14]

## "Civil Disobedience" Is Published

In 1849, Elizabeth Peabody included Thoreau's "Resistance to Civil Government" in the *Aesthetic Papers*. The title of the essay later was changed to "Civil Disobedience." It was based in part on Thoreau's experience in the Concord jail when he refused to pay the poll tax. He said, "Under a government which imprisons any unjustly, the true place for a just man is also a prison."[15]

This essay is one of Thoreau's greatest works. In it, he showcased his beliefs about the relationship between the individual and his government. Early in the essay, he said, "that government governs best that governs least." In other words, government should only perform the functions needed, and not try to run the lives of the people. In Thoreau's opinion, government is there "to protect the individual's freedom—his right to live in the manner he chooses without interference from others."[16]

He then describes the individual's obligation to the state, saying, "The only obligation which I have a right to assume, is to do at any time what I think right." Here he tells of his belief that the individual should be able to decide what is right, and if that conflicts with the law, then he or she should break the law.[17]

When the essay first appeared, it attracted little attention, but through the years, it has influenced such diverse world leaders as Mohandas Gandhi and Martin Luther King, Jr.

In the fall of 1849, the year "Civil Disobedience" was published, the Thoreau family moved from the house in the Texas section of Concord to one on Main Street. They could afford a bigger house because the pencil business was going well.

## Fugitive Slave Law Enacted

In 1851, Thoreau's antislavery feelings were strengthened when the Fugitive Slave Law was enacted. The federal government already had the authority to seize runaway slaves and send them back to their masters in the south. This new law imposed heavy penalties on people who helped a slave escape or interfered with a slave's recovery.

Emerson, usually gentle and law abiding, wrote in his journal, "I will not obey it, by God."[18] Thoreau suggested painting the Concord Monument black in mourning.

In Boston, an escaped slave named Fred Wilkins was working as a waiter. He was taken to court, and during a delay in the proceedings, was hustled out of the room and taken to Concord. The Thoreaus sheltered him until he could be taken to Canada. Once a slave reached Canada, he or she was safe, as there was a treaty in effect with Canada.

## Thoreau's Stand Against Slavery

The whole Thoreau family was abolitionist, meaning that they wanted slavery made illegal in the United States. Thoreau's mother and Aunt Maria were charter members of the Concord chapter of the Women's Anti-Slavery Society. His sisters were also active, as was Prudence Ward. Thoreau never joined an abolitionist organization, but he was always against slavery. He felt sympathy for all downtrodden people and continued to fight against slavery all his life.

Thoreau was against slavery not only in opinion, but he was also willing to work against it. He was a conductor on the Underground Railroad, which was a system for getting runaway slaves from the South to the northern states or Canada. People who helped the runaways were called conductors. Thoreau helped to hide numerous slaves in the family home. He often bought them tickets to Canada and escorted them to the train. In October, Thoreau wrote in his journal that he had put a fugitive slave on the train bound for Canada. By doing so, he was risking a great deal. He could have been fined or put in jail if he had been caught.

## Another Trip to Maine

In September 1853, Thoreau went back to Maine with his cousin, George Thatcher. Thatcher wanted to go moose hunting. Thoreau thought:

> this hunting of the moose merely for the satisfaction of killing him, not even for the sake of his hide, without making any extraordinary exertion or running any risk yourself, is too much like going out by night to some wood-side pasture and shooting your neighbor's horses. These are God's own horses, poor, timid creatures, that will run fast enough as soon as they smell you, though they are nine feet high.[19]

The account of this trip would become part of *The Maine Woods*, which would be published after Thoreau's death.

# 10

# PUBLISHING AND MORE TRAVEL

In March 1854, the publisher Ticknor and Fields accepted *Walden* and published the book at its expense. On March 28, Thoreau received the first batch of proofs to be corrected. The publisher sent them in small batches, and Thoreau worked on them all spring. He made lots of changes, noting, "When I have sent off my manuscripts to the printer, certain objectionable sentences and expressions are sure to obtrude themselves on my attention with force, though I had not consciously suspected them before."[1] He even added notes from his journal as late as April 27.

The first printed copy arrived on August 2. A two-inch announcement of the book's publication appeared in the *New York Tribune*. It was widely reviewed, and some reviews were very favorable.

# WALDEN;

OR,

# LIFE IN THE WOODS.

By HENRY D. THOREAU,

AUTHOR OF "A WEEK ON THE CONCORD AND MERRIMACK RIVERS."

I do not propose to write an ode to dejection, but to brag as lustily as chanticleer in the morning, standing on his roost, if only to wake my neighbors up. — Page 92.

BOSTON:

TICKNOR AND FIELDS.

M DCCC LIV.

*This is the title page to the original edition of Henry David Thoreau's* Walden, *published in 1854.*

However, the book was not a big success, selling only about two thousand copies in Thoreau's lifetime. The next year, he received a royalty check for $51.60.

## Walden

The book was divided into eighteen chapters, each of them devoted to a topic. Some chapters, like "Economy" and "Higher Laws," give arguments for simplicity and living close to nature. Others, like "The Ponds" and "The Beanfield," are more descriptive.

In *Walden*, Thoreau calls each person to live out his dream. This takes courage if your dream is not the same as the dreams of those around you. He believed that most people "lead lives of quiet desperation" because they accept the norm and do not follow their dreams.[2]

He wanted to show that people have the wrong idea of economics and what is necessary to live a good life. He maintains a man should not have to spend most of his time working to get what he needs to live. He says if you decide to be satisfied with less, you will have plenty of time to enjoy life.

He shows what life close to nature is like and the rewards it offers. Many passages describe everything from the beauty of the snow to the singing of birds to the actions of a fox in winter.

Thoreau's transcendental beliefs come through when he shows how his closer association with nature gives him a fuller life. He claimed that, "My profession is always on the alert to find God in nature, to know his lurking-places, to attend all the oratorios, the operas, in nature."[3]

## Opinions of *Walden*

Thoreau's friends were happy *Walden* was published, but they had different reactions to the book. Channing did not like it. Bronson Alcott was fascinated by it and wrote in his diary that the book would bring its author fame. He was right, although most of the fame did not come during Thoreau's lifetime. Emerson wrote, "All American kind are delighted with *Walden*."[4]

Once the book was published, Thoreau felt a sort of aimlessness. He had concentrated so much effort on the writing of *Walden* that he was not sure what to do next. It was a very hot summer. He had to "sit below with the family at evening" since it was too hot in his attic room to write. He complained in his journal about his lack of privacy.[5]

## New Friends

The publication of *Walden* brought Thoreau some new friends. Daniel Ricketson, a Quaker and abolitionist from New Bedford, wrote to him. He informed the author that he had tried all his life "to live as free from the restraint of mere forms and ceremonies as I possibly can."[6] He had built a small, cozy building on the grounds of his home where he entertained friends and enjoyed nature.

Thoreau answered, writing: "Yours is the only word of greeting I am likely to receive from a dweller in the woods like myself—from where the whippoorwill

*Daniel Ricketson created this likeness of his friend Henry David Thoreau.*

and cuckoo are heard, and there are . . . real breezes blowing."[7] Thus began a lifelong correspondence between the two men. Ricketson was not Thoreau's intellectual equal, but he had a merry disposition and a real love of nature.

Another new friend was an Englishman, Thomas Cholmondeley. Cholmondeley had just returned from New Zealand and had written a book about it. He came to see Emerson but boarded with the Thoreaus. Henry invited him to climb Mount Wachusett with him and his friends from Worcester. When Cholmondeley returned to London, he sent Thoreau twenty-four volumes of American Indian history and

**A Visit to Daniel Ricketson**

Daniel Ricketson wrote of Thoreau's arrival on Christmas Day, 1854:

> I had expected him at noon, but as he did not arrive, I had given him up for the day. In the latter part of the afternoon I was clearing off the snow from my front steps, when, looking up, I saw a man walking up the carriage road, bearing a portmanteau [suitcase] in one hand and an umbrella in the other. He was dressed in a long overcoat of a dark color and wore a dark soft hat. I had no suspicion it was Thoreau, and rather supposed it was a peddler of small wares.[8]

His disappointment at Thoreau's quaint-looking appearance was overcome by his conversation at the dinner table and a new friendship was formed.

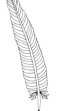

philosophy. Thoreau was familiar with many of the books and was very pleased to own them.

In September 1854, Samuel Worcester Rowse, a young portrait painter from Maine, stayed with the Thoreaus. Henry's mother asked him to do a crayon portrait of her son. Rowse caught the gentle expression and open quality of Thoreau's face as others had not.

Frank Sanborn was new to Concord that fall. The Harvard senior came to visit Emerson but became friends with Thoreau. He was an abolitionist and became one of Thoreau's first biographers. Later Sanborn came to Concord to teach. He thought Thoreau looked like "a sort of wise, wild beast." He said his "ruddy weather-beaten face . . . reminds me of some shrewd and honest animal's—some retired philosophical woodchuck or magnanimous [considerate or generous] fox."[9]

## Kansas-Nebraska Act

Slavery issues were heating up in 1854. Stephen A. Douglas, senator from Illinois, had introduced a bill in Congress to open the Nebraska and Kansas Territories for settlement. Thoreau disagreed with the bill, since the United States had already given much of that territory to the American Indians through treaties. Douglas proposed that popular vote in the territories should decide whether or not to allow slavery. Those who were against the spread of slavery opposed the bill, because it went against an earlier law—the Missouri

Compromise of 1820—which said there would be no slavery in the territories.

The North threatened to ignore the Fugitive Slave Law if the bill passed. On May 24, Anthony Burns, a runaway slave, was arrested in Boston. Congress passed the Kansas-Nebraska Act on May 25, and the next day, a mob of Bostonians tried to rescue Burns from the courthouse. They failed, but it took forty thousand dollars, twenty-two companies of the state militia, the sheriff's posse, four platoons of marines, and a battalion of U.S. artillery to return him to slavery.

Thoreau immediately wrote a lecture on unfair laws. He delivered it on July 4 at Framingham, Massachusetts. He said the question was not whether the Fugitive Slave Law was constitutional, but whether it was right. He said the law was wrong and should not be obeyed, but he stopped short of advocating violence.

## Speaking and Writing

Thoreau made a quick trip to Philadelphia in November to give his moose-hunting talk, stopping to see Greeley in New York on his way back. In December, he came up with a new talk, called "Life Without Principle." His main point was that spending your time working hard to get money would not necessarily bring fulfillment to your life. He gave the same lecture in Providence, Rhode Island; New Bedford, Massachusetts; and Nantucket that month. Thoreau wrote in his journal on December 6 that lecturing was a waste of time and art. "I would rather write books than lectures."[10]

The winter of 1854–1855 was unusually cold, and the rivers were frozen solid by December 19. The next day, Thoreau and Channing went skating. Thoreau described his friend, who did not have his skill at skating. He said that Channing's sweat "actually dropped from his forehead onto the ice, and it froze in long icicles on his beard."[11] Thoreau loved skating, saying it made him feel "like a new creature, a deer perhaps."[12] One day that winter he skated thirty miles.

In 1855, he wrote in his journal that he wanted to live so that he got his enjoyment from common events, his daily walk, conversations with neighbors, and things he could perceive through his senses. "That man is the richest whose pleasures are the cheapest," he concluded.[13]

In the spring of 1855, Thoreau contracted with George William Curtis, who had helped raise his cabin, to publish the Cape Cod sketches in *Putnam's Magazine*. Curtis thought some of the remarks about Christianity and the Cape residents might offend some people, but he started publishing them anyway. Installments appeared in June, July, and August issues. Then Curtis decided not to publish the rest, since Thoreau refused to change anything.

## Thoreau Becomes Ill Again

In mid-April 1855 Thoreau had become very ill. He was too tired to do anything but lie down, he had a bad cough, and his knees were weak. It was December before he was really well again.

He wrote to Blake, "I should feel a little less ashamed if I could give any name to my disorder, but I cannot, and our doctor cannot help me to it."[14] This was probably the beginning of his battle with the family illness, tuberculosis.

Thoreau did manage a trip to Cape Cod with Channing in July. They stayed with the keeper of the Highland Lighthouse. However, Thoreau complained of being tired and having no strength in his legs. In early October, he was still weak enough to have to travel around the countryside in a wagon when he visited Ricketson.

By November, Thoreau felt much better, saying he felt his "power of observation and contemplation is much increased."[15]

## Winter 1856

During the winter of 1856, Thoreau marveled at the snowflakes drifting down around him. "How full of creative genius is the air in which these are generated . . . Nature is full of genius, full of the divinity so that not a snowflake escapes its fashioning hand."[16] As always, he took pleasure in the common, ordinary things around him.

In March, Thoreau's Uncle Charlie Dunbar died. He wrote, "He was born in February, 1780, the winter of the Great Snow, and he died in the winter of another great snow—a life bounded by great snows."[17]

## Job Opportunities

Early in 1856, Thoreau lectured in Worcester and New Bedford. Greeley invited him to come live with his family at Chappaqua, New York, near New York City.[18] Greeley wanted Thoreau to serve as tutor for the Greeley children. Thoreau considered the move for several months but finally decided against it. He apparently did not want to live in the city again, and although he felt honored by Greeley's request, he did not want to lose touch with Concord and his home.

In September, Thoreau went to Walpole, New Hampshire, to visit Bronson Alcott, who had recently moved there. Alcott was involved in helping to plan an experimental cooperative community at Eagleswood, near Perth Amboy, New Jersey. They needed a surveyor and lecturer, so he recommended Thoreau, who accepted the position.

## Meeting With Walt Whitman

In November, Thoreau and Alcott went to call on Walt Whitman, who had published his book of poems, *Leaves of Grass*, the year before. Emerson had sent Whitman a congratulatory letter, ending: "I greet you at the beginning of a great career."[19]

Whitman and Thoreau were rather wary of one another. Thoreau did not think much of America and said so. Whitman was shocked. Alcott later wrote in his journal, ". . . each seemed planted fast in reserves, surveying the other curiously—like two wild beasts, each wondering what the other would do, whether to snap or run."[20] They later came to value one another's work.

Thoreau returned home late in November and continued his nature study. He said, "We must go out and re-ally ourselves to Nature every day . . . I am sensible that I am imbibing health when I open my mouth to the wind. Staying in the house breeds a kind of insanity always."[21]

## John Brown Comes to Concord

In March 1857, Thoreau met John Brown, a radical abolitionist who believed in using violence to bring about change. Brown came to see abolitionist Frank Sanborn and collect money for his cause. Sanborn took him to dinner at the Thoreaus', and Henry was quite impressed.

In June, Thoreau took his last trip to Cape Cod. William Ellery Channing was supposed to go but

backed out at the last minute. Thoreau went alone. He walked the last fifty-some miles to the Headland Light where he stayed. The Cape was entirely different from the tourist

*Though Henry Thoreau preferred nonviolent resistance, he greatly respected fellow abolitionist John Brown (pictured).*

attraction it is today. There were only a few small hotels, and residents barely managed to make a living from the sea. Thoreau was excellent at describing the people and customs in his book, *Cape Cod*. It is still stocked in gift shops on Cape Cod today.

## A Third Trip to Maine

Before he had been home a month, Thoreau was planning a third trip to Maine. He and Edward Hoar hired Joe Polis, a Penobscot Indian, as a guide and set off on a 325-mile canoe trip.

It was a difficult journey. The men had to fight insects, battle high winds and waves as they crossed lakes, and carry the canoe around numerous obstacles. They were wet most of the time, sometimes they were lost, and Edward was separated from the other two overnight once. Thoreau frantically wondered how he would tell Ed's parents if they never found him. He wrote Blake that their best nights had been the ones when it rained hard, because it cut down on the mosquitoes.

Thoreau called his account of the trip "The Allegash and East Branch," but it was mostly about Joe Polis. Thoreau was fascinated by the man, who was an important figure in his tribe. Polis had represented his tribe in Washington, D.C., and had met Daniel Webster, a famous statesman. Polis was a Christian who prayed often, yet he retained his people's ways of the woods. Thoreau learned some American Indian language from him, as well as American Indian names for many plants.

## Thoreau's Scientific Interests

Thoreau's interests were becoming more scientific, and he was interested in botany, zoology, geology, and geography. He was a corresponding member of the Boston Society of Natural History.

The fall of 1857 was a beautiful one, lasting well into November. Thoreau reveled in the season and wrote some important parts of his essay "Autumnal Tints." He lectured about fall, speaking in front of a white background with autumn leaves mounted on it. October and March were his favorite months, as he loved the changing of the seasons.

In 1858, Thoreau's narrative of his second Maine expedition, called "Chesuncook," appeared in the *Atlantic Monthly*. Writing about a pine tree, he said, "It is the living spirit of the tree, not its spirit of turpentine, with which I sympathize, and which heals my cuts. It is as immortal as I am, and perchance will go to as high a heaven, there to tower above me still."[22] Thoreau considered nature to be equal with people.

James Russell Lowell, now editor of the *Atlantic Monthly*, removed the part about the pine tree going to heaven. Thoreau was angry, and Lowell did not publish any of his work again.

## More Travel

Early in the summer of 1858, Thoreau went to Mount Monadnock with Harrison Blake. They spent two nights on the mountain.

The next month, Thoreau and Edward Hoar traveled to the White Mountains with Theo Brown and

*Ralph Waldo Emerson (pictured) and Henry Thoreau did not get along that well later in life.*

Harrison Blake. They asked a tavern keeper about a guide one foggy morning. They wanted to visit Tuckerman's Ravine on Mount Washington. The tavern keeper's brother was a guide, but he said he could not go out in fog like that. Thoreau, using his compass and a map, figured out how to get to the ravine, where he fell and sprained his ankle. He treated it with a plant, *Arnica mollis*.

## Friendship With Emerson Cools

During the 1850s, Thoreau's friendship with Emerson was strained. Emerson thought Thoreau should be more successful in literature, and Thoreau criticized Emerson for being too refined. He wrote, "Talked, or tried to talk, with R.W.E. [Ralph Waldo Emerson] Lost my time—nay, almost my identity."[23] Emerson wrote about him, "If I knew only Thoreau, I should think cooperation of good men impossible."[24]

# 11

# THE LAST
# YEARS

A s the 1850s drew to a close, Henry Thoreau was
living at home with his mother, his sister Sophia,
and his father, who was seriously ill.

## Father's Illness and Death

Late in 1858, Thomas Cholmondeley wrote Henry
Thoreau from Montreal, asking him to travel to the
West Indies with him. Thoreau refused, since he did
not want to leave his sick father.

John Thoreau, Sr., was confined to his room from
the middle of January 1859. Henry and Sophia helped
their mother take care of him. Cynthia Thoreau said
she had never seen such tenderness from her son.[1]

On February 3, John Thoreau died after a two-year
illness. Henry wrote in his journal that day, "Five minutes

before 3 P.M., Father died."[2] He left the rest of the page blank, then used several pages to describe his father's illness and his love for Concord.

## Business

With his father gone, Henry David Thoreau was in charge of the family business and spent many hours filling orders and doing the paperwork his father had always done. He did not have time to travel much.

Thoreau did a lot of surveying. A group of local farmers asked him to do a study of the Sudbury and Concord rivers, which were backing up and flooding their meadows. This study took six weeks and resulted in a map inscribed: "Henry. D. Thoreau, Civil Engineer."[3]

Thoreau lectured in 1859, but after one lecture, he wrote, "There can be no good reading unless there is good hearing also. It takes two at least for this game, as for love, and they must cooperate."[4] Still, he continued to lecture in Worcester, Concord, and Boston that year.

## John Brown and Harpers Ferry

News came in October of John Brown's raid on the U.S. arsenal at Harpers Ferry. Brown had planned to start a republic for free slaves in the Appalachians. This would serve as a base from which he would fight against the slave states. Harpers Ferry was the first step in his plan, but things went wrong. Ten of Brown's twenty-two men were killed, including both of his

*This illustration shows the capture of John Brown (bearded man on ground at right) and his followers at Harpers Ferry.*

sons. Brown was captured, along with six others, and arrested on October 16, 1859. Five men escaped.[5]

Thoreau immediately began writing about Brown, pouring out ten thousand words in a few days. He was totally obsessed with Brown during this time. He later recalled that he slept with pencil and paper under his pillow. "When I could not sleep," he said, "I wrote in the dark."[6]

Brown's trial was to begin on October 27, and Thoreau wanted to finish and deliver his speech before a verdict was reached. He spoke in Concord on October 30, calling his talk "A Plea for Captain John Brown." The meeting was in the Universalist Church. Emerson reported that everyone in the audience was respectful, and many were surprisingly moved by Thoreau's speech.[7]

## Thoreau's Defense of Brown

Thoreau defended Brown for standing up for his principles. Speaking of Brown, Thoreau said, "It was his peculiar doctrine that a man has a perfect right to interfere by force with the slave-holder, in order to rescue the slave. I agree with him."[8] Thoreau delivered the same lecture in Boston and Worcester during the next few days. After many years of backing nonviolence, Thoreau was finally beginning to think that it might be necessary to use force to end slavery.

Brown was found guilty and sentenced to be hanged on December 2. Thoreau held a memorial service for him in the town hall the day he was executed. The same day, Thoreau helped transport a fugitive slave from Harpers Ferry to Canada.

On April 3, Frank Sanborn was arrested by federal marshals because he had had prior knowledge of the raid at Harpers Ferry. His arrest made the front page of the *New York Tribune*. Townspeople in Concord were sympathetic and gave him a hero's welcome when he was released by a state court in Boston.

A memorial service was planned for John Brown in North Elba, New York, on July 4, 1860. Thoreau was invited to speak but declined. However, he sent some remarks to be read. They were printed in *The Liberator*, an abolitionist magazine, with the title, "The Last Days of John Brown."

## Later Writing

In July 1860, Henry Thoreau and Ellery Channing spent almost a week on Mount Monadnock. This was Channing's first canoeing trip, and he found himself on top of a mountain, drenched in a summer rain. Thoreau was not bothered at all but went about the business of building a shelter of spruce boughs. He was trying to learn more about the alpine environment, and he took lots of notes.

Since March, Thoreau had been reorganizing his journals, categorizing all the seasonal phenomena he had written about. He would work on this for the next twenty-two months.

In September, Thoreau discovered a rare Canadian lynx, a type of wildcat, that had been killed near town. This discovery provided for several long journal entries, and he wrote about it for the Boston Society of Natural History.

## Interest in Forests

Thoreau became interested in forests and how they grow, including the ways in which seeds are dispersed, or spread. He wrote that seed-eating birds and squirrels, rather than destroying life, actually help seeds to disperse and grow into trees.

Although allergies had not been discovered yet, Thoreau had ideas on the subject. He wrote, "Who knows but the pollen of some plants may be unwholesome to inhale, and produce the diseases of the season?"[9]

Also, he gave a talk on the "Succession of Forest Trees" at the Middlesex Agricultural Society in September 1860. The lecture was printed in the *New York Tribune*, two official reports, and a farming journal, making it his most-published article during his lifetime.

Thoreau began trying to determine the ages of trees by counting the rings on a cross-section of each tree's trunk. In November 1860, he found a cedar tree that had been alive before Europeans started settling in New England in the early 1600s.

## Thoreau's Last Illness

On December 3, 1860, Thoreau spent a good deal of time on a wet day counting the rings on a tree. He became ill with a severe cold, which later became bronchitis, a sickness of the lungs. He was sick all winter, and his journal suffered. He was too ill for a while to write, and he could not get outside to observe nature.

His friends Harry Blake and Theo Brown came to visit him that winter, and he managed to keep up his end of the conversation despite being sick.

The Civil War began that spring when the southern states seceded, or withdrew from the Union because of disagreements over slavery. Thoreau was too ill to take much interest in it, despite his strong stance against slavery.

By April 1861, the doctors recommended that he go to the West Indies, which he thought was too muggy, or the south of Europe, which he said cost too much in both time and money. He decided to go to Minnesota instead, where he could see how American Indians lived and study grassland plants.

## A Trip to Minnesota

Neither Channing nor Blake was able to go with him, so seventeen-year-old Horace Mann, Jr., son of the great educator Horace Mann, offered to go. They traveled by railroad and steamboat.

It was a difficult journey, and although Thoreau got to see Chicago, Illinois, St. Paul, Minnesota, an American Indian dance and ceremony, and the Mississippi River, he did not write much. He took notes on natural history, with Mann's help, but never had a chance to transcribe the notes into his journal as he wanted to.

Emerson's Chicago friend Reverend Robert Collyer saw Thoreau and said, "he would hesitate for an instant now and then, waiting for the right word, or would pause with a pathetic patience to master the trouble in his chest."[10] When Thoreau came home, he was in even worse health than before. The family curse of tuberculosis was catching up with him. He had probably had it for several years. The disease was a common killer in Concord.

In August, 1861, Thoreau wrote to Ricketson that he had been sick so long, he had almost forgotten how it felt to be well. He visited his friend one last time. While he was there, a photographer named Dunshee took his picture. It shows a sad, tired man, looking much older than forty-four.

## End of the Journal

In September, Thoreau tried to get back into the habit of making journal entries. He wrote about the antics of a playful kitten. In October, he wrote only about the birds he could see from the window and stories that visitors told him.

His last journal entry was written on November 3, 1861, after walking to the railroad tracks. He wrote a graphic description of the way the heavy rain had marked the gravel. His last entry ended, "All this is perfectly distinct to an observant eye, and yet could easily pass unnoticed by most. Thus each wind is self-registering."[11] He meant that those who are observant notice things that most people miss, and everything leaves its mark.

## Thoreau Sells More Articles

In the last months of 1861, Thoreau cleared up outstanding debts with the customers of the pencil business. He also worked on selling some articles.

James T. Fields, now editor of the *Atlantic Monthly*, asked him to send some of his lectures to be printed. Thoreau agreed, if Fields would send him proofs and not alter anything without his consent. He also wanted to retain copyright of the articles. That way, no one else could republish them without his permission. He revised "Autumnal Tints," "Walking," and "Life Without Principle."

Fields decided to use "Walking" first, but Thoreau would never see it in print.

**Thoreau on Walking**

In an excerpt from "Walking" as printed in *Atlantic Monthly*, Thoreau explains that one must be completely free of responsibilities in order to be ready to go on a long walk in the wilderness: "If you are ready to leave father and mother, and brother and sister, and wife and child and friends, and never see them again; if you have paid your debts, and made your will, and settled all your affairs, and are a free man; then you are ready for a walk."[12]

## Thoreau's Last Months

By the beginning of 1862, everyone knew Henry Thoreau was dying. He wrote in a letter to a new admirer on March 21, "If I were to live, I should have much to report on Natural History generally," but he added, "I *suppose* that I have not many months to live."[13]

He spent his last few months surrounded by his family and friends. He had his bed brought down from the attic room so he could visit with friends and family. Sophia was devoted to him, and when he became too weak to write, she wrote for him.

Sam Staples, his former jailer, came to visit him in his last days. Staples met Emerson as he was leaving, and told him he had never seen a man dying "with so much pleasure and peace."[14]

Aunt Maria was concerned about her nephew's soul and asked if he had made his peace with God. Thoreau replied, "I did not know we had ever quarrelled, Aunt."[15]

A family friend and fellow abolitionist Parker Pillsbury stopped in to see Thoreau. He said, "You seem so near the brink of the dark river that I almost wonder how the opposite shore may appear to you."[16] Thoreau looked at him and replied, "One world at a time."[17]

The last month, he was only able to speak in a whisper. His mother and sister surrounded him with flowers, pictures, and books. On nights when he could not sleep, they set a candlelit lamp on the floor so he could watch the flickering shadows. He was weak, but he was aware of what was going on around him till the end.

Thoreau was awake early on the morning of May 6, 1862. Judge Rockwood Hoar brought him a bouquet of hyacinths from his garden, and Thoreau was pleased. Another friend came by soon with a dish of jelly.

Thoreau wanted to work on revising *A Week on the Concord and Merrimack Rivers*, so Sophia read to him from it, finishing the chapter entitled "Thursday." Anticipating the account of their quick trip home in the next chapter, he whispered, "Now comes good sailing."[18] A few minutes later he spoke his last sentence, but the only words the Thoreaus could understand were "moose" and "Indian."[19] He was apparently talking about the *Maine Woods* book.

At 9:00 on the morning of May 6, 1862, Thoreau died peacefully, with his mother, his sister Sophia, and Aunt Maria beside him.

## Thoreau's Friends Remember Him

Just before 3:00 on the afternoon of May 9, the bells tolled at the First Parish Church, and the church filled up with mourners for Henry David Thoreau. His best friends were there—people like William Ellery Channing, Bronson Alcott, Ralph Waldo Emerson, and Nathaniel Hawthorne. Emerson spoke, saying, "No truer American existed than Thoreau." He ended by saying, "His soul was made for the noblest society; he had in a short life exhausted the capabilities of this world; wherever there is knowledge, wherever there is virtue, wherever there is beauty, he will find a home."[20]

Thoreau was buried first in the family plot in the New Burying Ground in Concord. Later his body was moved to Sleepy Hollow Cemetery on Bedford Road in Concord. His grave is surrounded by the graves of Bronson Alcott, William Ellery Channing, Ralph Waldo Emerson, and Nathaniel Hawthorne. The inscription on his grave stone reflects the simplicity with which he tried to live his live: It merely reads "HENRY."

# 12

# THOREAU'S LEGACY

**H**enry David Thoreau's legacy is much more apparent now than it was during his own time. His writings have influenced many people through the ages— ordinary people as well as some world-famous figures.

## Impact on His Friends

Thoreau's friend Ricketson showed his appreciation to Thoreau just before he died, writing, "Your works, and above all, your brave and truthful life, will become a precious treasure."[1]

One of his former students, Louisa May Alcott, based Adam Warwick, the hero of her first novel *Moods* on Thoreau. She made Warwick a wandering scholar who is devoted to nature and is satisfied with few material things.

Edward Emerson, son of Ralph Waldo Emerson, wrote in his biography of Thoreau, "Our woods and waters will always be different because of this man. Something of him abides and truly 'for good' in his town. Here he was born, and within its borders he found a wealth of beauty and interest—all that he asked—and shared it with us all."[2]

## Exposure of His Writings After His Death

As soon as Thoreau died, his works gained more exposure. *Atlantic Monthly* published seven of his articles in the two and a half years after his death. They also published Emerson's funeral oration and a tribute written by Bronson Alcott.

Ticknor and Fields brought out a collection of travel essays entitled *Excursions in Field and Forest* in 1863, *The Maine Woods* in 1864, *Cape Cod* and *Letters to Various Persons* in 1865, and *A Yankee in Canada with Anti-Slavery and Reform Papers* in 1866.

The first biography of Thoreau, *Thoreau: The Poet Naturalist*, by William Ellery Channing, was published in 1873. Frank Sanborn's biography came out in 1882.

In the 1880s, Thoreau became recognized as America's foremost nature writer. Harry Blake published four volumes of selections from Thoreau's journals, based on the four seasons, between 1881 and 1892. Thoreau was one of the first to realize conservation was necessary in the United States. Twentieth century naturalist John Burroughs used many quotes from Thoreau in his first book.

## Thoreau and Religion

Some thought Thoreau did not believe in any god because of his break with the established church. However, he was deeply religious in his own way. He referred to God as "the Artist who made the world and me," "the Maker of this earth," and "the greater Benefactor and Intelligence that stands over me. . . ."[3] Thoreau held the transcendentalist view that one should learn about God by reasoning, not by following the established church.

## Influence of Thoreau's Writings

Other countries were also beginning to recognize Thoreau. A biography of Thoreau by Henry S. Salt, a British biographer, was published in London in 1890. Also, the Labour Party units in England were referred to as Walden Clubs. A Dutch translation of *Walden* came out in 1902. Russian novelist Leo Tolstoy called Thoreau one of "a bright constellation" of American writers "who . . . specially influenced me." He said Americans should pay more attention to Thoreau than to financiers and generals.[4]

In 1906, a twenty-volume collection of Thoreau's works was published. In the early twentieth century, people began to realize that, in addition to being a nature writer, Thoreau was also an important social and political thinker. Writer and political reformer Upton Sinclair and political candidate Norman Thomas were arrested for reading from "Civil Disobedience" in public. Sinclair was a novelist, and

*The original site of Henry Thoreau's cabin was discovered by Roland Wells Robbins on November 11, 1945. A sign beside the site quotes Thoreau: "I went to the woods because I wished to live deliberately, to front only the essential facts of life. And see if I could not learn what it had to teach and not, when I came to die, discover that I had not lived."*

Thomas ran for president of the United States six times.

The controversy over Thoreau's writing continued. As late as the 1950s, Senator Joseph McCarthy succeeded in having Thoreau's writings removed from the U.S. Information Service libraries throughout the world. McCarthy spent years accusing government officials and others of being Communists—believers in an economic system where the government is supposed to evenly distribute property and goods among the people. Apparently he thought Thoreau's writings showed Communist tendencies.

Finally a series of hearings, called the Army-McCarthy hearings, were held. McCarthy was accusing the Secretary of the Army of protecting Communists, so the special investigation was called for. The hearings were televised, and McCarthy lost his popularity with the public when they saw him bullying witnesses and making groundless accusations. Nothing was proved, and the Senate voted 67 to 22 to condemn McCarthy for improper conduct.

Along with being controversial, Thoreau's works also inspired many people. Mohandas Gandhi, later known for nonviolent resistance, was deeply impressed when he read "Civil Disobedience" in 1908. "The essay seemed to me so convincing and truthful," he wrote years later, "that I felt the need of knowing more of Thoreau."[5] Martin Luther King, Jr. gave Thoreau's "Civil Disobedience" credit for inspiring his civil rights campaigns in the South, which were aimed at getting equal treatment for African Americans.

## Thoreau Today

In the beginning of the twenty-first century, people continue to read and be influenced by Thoreau's writings. *Walden* and "Civil Disobedience" are routinely studied today in high schools and universities across the country. Thoreau's journals are some of his most popular writings, and have helped many people draw closer to nature and a personal sense of peace.

# CHRONOLOGY

1817—Born in Concord, Massachusetts, on July 12.

1818—Family moves to Chelmsford.

1821—Family moves to Boston.

1823—Family moves back to Concord.

1828—Is enrolled in Concord Academy.

1833—Enters Harvard University.

1835—Teaches one term in Canton, Massachusetts.

1837—Graduates from Harvard; Teaches in Concord School a few days; Begins journal on October 22.

1838—Gives first lecture on April 11; Opens private school in home in June.

1839—Meets Ellen Sewall on July 20; Takes trip on river with brother, John, in September.

1840—Has poem and essay published in *The Dial*; Proposes to Ellen and she refuses.

1841—School closes because of John's illness; Moves in with Emersons in April.

1842—John dies on January 11; Wallie Emerson dies on January 27; Meets Nathaniel Hawthorne; *The Dial* prints eight of Thoreau's poems.

1843—Goes to Staten Island as tutor; Meets Horace Greeley; Moves home in December.

1844—Accidentally sets fire to Concord Woods with Edward Hoar.

1845—Builds cabin at Walden Pond and moves in July 4.

1846—Is jailed for not paying poll taxes; First trip to Maine.

1847—Leaves Walden in September; Moves back in with Emersons.

1849—Publishes "Resistance to Civil Government"; Publishes *A Week on the Concord and Merrimack Rivers*; Sister Helen dies; Goes to Cape Cod.

1850—Takes trip to Canada.

1853—Three installments of *Excursion to Canada* published; Goes to Maine again.

1854—*Walden* is published.

1855—Is ill most of the year; Takes trip to Cape Cod anyway.

1856—Goes to Perth Amboy, New Jersey, as surveyor and lecturer; Meets Walt Whitman.

1857—Meets John Brown; Goes to Cape Cod alone; Goes to Maine woods.

1858—Takes trip to White Mountains.

1859—Father dies on February 3; Speaks on John Brown and has memorial service for him.

1860—Goes to Mount Monadnock in August; Becomes ill December 3.

1861—Is ill all year; Travels to Minnesota for his health May 11–July 10.

1862—Dies at home on May 6.

# CHAPTER NOTES

### Chapter 1. A Night in Jail

1. Henry David Thoreau, *The Selected Works of Thoreau, Civil Disobedience* (Boston: Houghton Mifflin Company, 1975), p. 804.

2. Ibid., pp. 802–803.

3. Harmon Smith, *My Friend, My Friend* (Amherst: University of Massachusetts Press, 1999), p. 105.

4. Thoreau, p. 803.

5. Henry Beetle Hough, *Thoreau of Walden* (New York: Simon & Schuster, 1956), p. 147.

6. Ibid., p. 146.

7. Smith, p. 106.

8. Henry Seidel Canby, *Thoreau* (Boston: Houghton Mifflin Company, 1939), p. 234.

9. Thoreau, p. 792.

10. William Cain, *A Historical Guide to Henry David Thoreau* (New York: Oxford University Press, 2000), p. 36.

11. Canby, p. 235.

### Chapter 2. Growing Up in Concord

1. William Ellery Channing, *Thoreau: The Poet Naturalist* (Boston: Roberts Brothers, 1873), p. 1.

2. Henry Seidel Canby, *Thoreau* (Boston: Houghton Mifflin Company, 1939), p. 8.

3. Henry Beetle Hough, *Thoreau of Walden* (New York: Simon & Schuster, 1956), pp. 24–25.

4. Edward Waldo Emerson, *Henry Thoreau, as Remembered by a Young Friend* (Boston: Houghton Mifflin Company, 1917), pp. 14–15.

5. Hildegarde Hawthorne, *Concord's Happy Rebel* (New York: Longman's Green & Company, 1940), p. 23.

6. Douglas T. Miller, *Henry David Thoreau: A Man for All Seasons* (New York: Facts on File, 1991), p. 14.

7. Ibid.

8. Canby, p. 28.

9. Hough, p. 15.

10. F. B. Sanborn, *The Life of Henry David Thoreau* (Boston & New York: Houghton Mifflin Company, 1917), p. 22.

11. Hough, p. 28.

12. Joseph Wood Krutch, *Henry David Thoreau* (New York: W. Sloane Associates, 1948), p. 19.

## Chapter 3. The Harvard Years

1. Robert Kuhn McGregor, *A Wider View of the Universe: Henry Thoreau's Study of Nature* (Chicago: University of Illinois Press, 1997), p. 8.

2. Robert D. Richardson, *Henry David Thoreau: A Life of the Mind* (Berkeley: University of California Press, 1980), p. 11.

3. Ibid.

4. Ibid., p. 9.

5. Henry Beetle Hough, *Thoreau of Walden* (New York: Simon & Schuster, 1956), p. 36.

6. Ibid., p. 39.

7. August Derleth, *Concord Rebel* (Philadelphia: Chilton Company, 1962), p. 12.

8. William Cain, *A Historical Guide to Henry David Thoreau* (New York: Oxford University Press, 2000), p. 14.

9. Douglas T. Miller, *Henry David Thoreau: A Man for All Seasons* (New York: Facts on File, 1991), pp. 21–22.

10. Ibid., p. 22.

11. Joseph Wood Krutch, *Henry David Thoreau* (New York: W. Sloane Associates, 1948), pp. 21–23.

12. Harmon Smith, *My Friend, My Friend* (Amherst: University of Massachusetts Press, 1999), p. 141.

13. Hough, p. 36.

14. Henry Seidel Canby, *Thoreau* (Boston: Houghton Mifflin Company, 1939), p. 50.

## Chapter 4. Thoreau's Teaching Career

1. Robert D. Richardson, *Henry Thoreau: A Life of the Mind* (Berkeley: University of California Press, 1986), p. 5.

2. Joseph Wood Krutch, *Henry David Thoreau* (New York: W. Sloane Associates, 1948), p. 29.

3. Harmon Smith, *My Friend, My Friend* (Amherst: University of Massachusetts Press, 1999), p. 15.

4. August Derleth, *Concord Rebel* (Philadelphia: Chilton Company, 1962), p. 19.

5. Richardson, p. 6.

6. Derleth, p. 18.

7. Ibid., p. 17.

8. Ibid., p. 19.

9. Smith, p. 28.

10. Hildegarde Hawthorne, *Concord's Happy Rebel* (New York: Longman's Green & Company, 1940), p. 53.

11. Henry Beetle Hough, *Thoreau of Walden* (New York: Simon & Schuster, 1956), p. 59.

## Chapter 5. A Trip on the River

1. Henry Beetle Hough, *Thoreau of Walden* (New York: Simon & Schuster, 1956), p. 74.

2. Ibid., p. 73.

3. August William Derleth, *Concord Rebel* (Philadelphia: Chilton Company, 1962), p. 26.

4. F. B. Sanborn, *The Life of Henry David Thoreau* (Boston & New York: Houghton Mifflin Company, 1917), pp. 224–225.

5. Robert D. Richardson, *Henry Thoreau: A Life of the Mind* (Berkeley: University of California Press, 1986), p. 65.

6. Hildegarde Hawthorne, *Concord's Happy Rebel* (New York: Longman's Green & Company, 1940), p. 61.

7. Hough, p. 76.

8. Richardson, p. 65.

## Chapter 6. Love and Publication

1. Joseph Wood Krutch, *Henry David Thoreau* (New York: W. Sloane Associates, 1948), p. 30.

2. Henry Beetle Hough, *Thoreau of Walden* (New York: Simon & Schuster, 1956), p. 77.

3. August William Derleth, *Concord Rebel* (Philadelphia: Chilton Company, 1962), p. 24.

4. Harmon Smith, *My Friend, My Friend* (Amherst: University of Massachusetts Press, 1999), p. 26.

5. Henry Seidel Canby, *Thoreau* (Boston: Houghton Mifflin Company, 1939), p. 112.

6. Derleth, p. 28.

7. Canby, p. 13.

8. Krutch, p. 31.

9. Hildegarde Hawthorne, *Concord's Happy Rebel* (New York: Longman's Green & Company, 1940), p. 65.

10. Canby, p. 118.

11. Robert D. Richardson, *Henry Thoreau: A Life of the Mind* (Berkeley: University of California Press, 1986), p. 62.

12. Ibid.

## Chapter 7. Writer, Lecturer, and Handyman

1. Joseph Wood Krutch, *Henry David Thoreau* (New York: W. Sloane Associates, 1948), p. 42.

2. Henry Seidel Canby, *Thoreau* (Boston: Houghton Mifflin Company, 1939), p. 174.

3. Robert D. Richardson, *Henry Thoreau: A Life of the Mind* (Berkeley: University of California Press, 1986), p. 112.

4. Hildegarde Hawthorne, *Concord's Happy Rebel* (New York: Longman's Green & Company, 1940), p. 74.

5. Henry Thoreau quoted in: Edward Waldo Emerson, "Henry Thoreau as Remembered by a Young Friend," n.d., <http://www.walden.org//contemporaries/E/Emerson_Edward_Waldo/HDT_Remembered_02.htm> (August 21, 2002).

6. Krutch, p. 44.

7. Henry Beetle Hough, *Thoreau of Walden* (New York: Simon & Schuster, 1956), p. 105.

8. Douglas T. Miller, *Henry David Thoreau: A Man for All Seasons* (New York: Facts on File, 1991), p. 32.

9. William L. Howarth, *The Book of Concord: Thoreau's Life as a Writer* (New York: Viking Press, 1982), p. 33.

10. Richardson, p. 127.

11. Ibid., p. 132.

12. Canby, p. 182.

13. Ibid., p. 175.

14. Hawthorne, p. 94.

## Chapter 8. At Walden Pond

1. Joseph Wood Krutch, *Henry David Thoreau* (New York: W. Sloane Associates, 1948), p. 53.

2. Henry David Thoreau, *The Annotated Walden* (New York: Barnes & Noble Books, 1992), p. 222.

3. Ibid., p. 177.

4. Ibid., p. 185.

5. Krutch, p. 79.

6. Henry Beetle Hough, *Thoreau of Walden* (New York: Simon & Schuster, 1956), pp. 135–136.

7. Douglas T. Miller, *Henry David Thoreau: A Man for All Seasons* (New York: Facts on File, 1981), p. 4.

8. Hough, p. 138.

9. Henry David Thoreau, "*Walden*: 2. Where I Lived and What I Lived for," *The Thoreau Reader*, July 9, 2002 <http://eserver.org/thoreau/walden02.html> (August 23, 2002).

10. Henry David Thoreau, "*Walden*: 8. The Village," *The Thoreau Reader*, July 9, 2002 <http://eserver.org/thoreau/walden08.html> (August 26, 2002).

11. Thoreau, *The Annotated Walden*, p. 299.

12. Ibid., p. 276.

13. Ibid.

14. Krutch, p. 56.

15. Ibid.

16. Ibid., p. 85.

17. Hildegarde Hawthorne, *Concord's Happy Rebel* (New York: Longman's Green & Company, 1940), pp. 95–96.

18. Hough, p. 152.

19. William L. Howarth, *The Book of Concord: Thoreau's Life as a Writer* (New York: Viking Press, 1982), p. 41.

20. Richard Lebeaux, *Thoreau's Seasons* (Amherst: University of Massachusetts Press, 1984), p. 45.

21. Thoreau, *The Annotated Walden*, p. 440.

## Chapter 9. Lecturing and Travel

1. Joseph Wood Krutch, *Henry David Thoreau* (New York: W. Sloane Associates, 1948), p. 87.

2. Henry David Thoreau, *The Correspondence of Henry David Thoreau* (New York: New York University, 1958), p. 189.

3. Ibid., pp. 190–191.

4. Ibid., p. 207.

5. Krutch, p. 98.

6. Douglas T. Miller, *Henry David Thoreau: A Man for All Seasons* (New York: Facts on File, 1991), p. 57.

7. Krutch, p. 102.

8. Hildegarde Hawthorne, *Concord's Happy Rebel* (New York: Longman's Green & Company, 1940), p. 115.

9. Ibid.

10. Henry Beetle Hough, *Thoreau of Walden* (New York: Simon & Schuster, 1956), p. 182.

11. Ibid., p. 165.

12. Krutch, p. 92.

13. Hough, p. 166.

14. Philip Gura, *The Cambridge Companion to Henry David Thoreau* (New York: Cambridge University Press, 1995), p. 149.

15. Hough, p. 163.

16. Len Gougeon, *The Cambridge Companion to Henry David Thoreau* (New York: Cambridge University Press, 1995), pp. 201–202.

17. Ibid., p. 202.

18. "Ralph Waldo Emerson: An outline Biography, Emerson and Transcendentalism," *age-of-the-sage.org*, n.d., <http://www.age-of-the-sage.org/ralph_waldo_emerson.html> (August 26, 2002).

19. Henry David Thoreau, *"Maine Woods*: Chesuncook–Part 3," *The Thoreau Reader*, July 9, 2002, <http://eserver.org/thoreau/chesck03.html> (August 26, 2002).

## Chapter 10. Publishing and More Travel

1. Robert D. Richardson, *Henry Thoreau: A Life of the Mind* (Berkeley: University of California Press, 1986), p. 313.

2. Ibid., p. 318.

3. Walter Harding, *The New Thoreau Handbook* (New York: New York University Press, 1980), pp. 124–125.

4. Joseph Wood Krutch, *Henry David Thoreau* (New York: W. Sloane Associates, 1948), p. 103.

5. Richardson, p. 323.

6. Ibid., p. 328.

7. Henry Beetle Hough, *Thoreau of Walden* (New York: Simon & Schuster, 1956), p. 214.

8. Ibid., p. 215.

9. Ibid., p. 220.

10. William L. Howarth, *The Book of Concord: Thoreau's Life as a Writer* (New York: Viking Press, 1982), p. 103.

11. Richardson, p. 334.

12. Ibid.

13. Krutch, p. 115.

14. Hough, p. 223.

15. Richardson, p. 340.

16. Ibid., p. 341.

17. Hough, p. 223.

18. Ibid., p. 227.

19. Richardson, p. 347.

20. Hough, p. 229.

21. Ibid., p. 230.

22. Henry David Thoreau, "*Maine Woods*: Chesuncook– Part 3," *The Thoreau Reader*, July 9, 2002, <http://eserver.org/thoreau/chesck03.html> (August 26, 2002).

23. Krutch, p. 226.

24. William Cain, *A Historical Guide to Henry David Thoreau* (New York: Oxford University Press, 2000), p. 40.

## Chapter 11. The Last Years

1. Robert Kuhn McGregor, *A Wider View of the Universe: Henry Thoreau's Study of Nature* (Chicago: University of Illinois Press, 1997), p. 176.

2. William L. Howarth, *The Book of Concord: Thoreau's Life as a Writer* (New York: Viking Press, 1982), p. 168.

3. Joseph Wood Krutch, *Henry David Thoreau* (New York: W. Sloane Associates, 1948), p. 221.

4. Howarth, p. 169.

5. "Harper's Ferry," *PBS Online*, n.d., <www.pbs.org/wgbh/aia/part4/4p2940.html> (August 26, 2002).

6. Henry David Thoreau, "A Plea for Captain John Brown by Henry David Thoreau; October 30, 1859," *The Avalon Project at Yale Law School*, n.d., <http://www.yale.edu/lawweb/avalon/treatise/thoreau/thoreau_001.htm> (August 26, 2002).

7. Henry Beetle Hough, *Thoreau of Walden* (New York: Simon & Schuster, 1956), p. 243.

8. Ibid.

9. Howarth, p. 190.

10. Robert D. Richardson, *Henry Thoreau: A Life of the Mind* (Berkeley: University of California Press, 1986), p. 387.

11. William Cain, *A Historical Guide to Henry David Thoreau* (New York: Oxford University Press, 2000), p. 131.

12. Henry David Thoreau, "Walking–Part 1 of 3," *The Thoreau Reader*, July 9, 2002, <http://eserver.org/thoreau/walking1.html> (August 26, 2002).

13. Richardson, p. 388.

14. Hough, p. 256.

15. Edward Waldo Emerson, *Henry Thoreau, as Remembered by a Young Friend* (Boston: Houghton Mifflin Company, 1917), p. 118.

16. Richardson, p. 389.

17. Ibid.

18. Howarth, p. 219.

19. Richardson, p. 389.

20. Harmon Smith, *My Friend, My Friend* (Amherst: University of Massachusetts Press, 1999), p. 183.

## Chapter 12. Thoreau's Legacy

1. William L. Howarth, *The Book of Concord: Thoreau's Life as a Writer* (New York: Viking Press, 1982), p. 218.

2. Edward Waldo Emerson, *Henry Thoreau, as Remembered by a Young Friend* (Boston: Houghton Mifflin Company, 1917), p. 118.

3. Edward Wagenknecht, *Henry David Thoreau: What Manner of Man?* (Amherst: The University of Massachusetts Press, 1981), p. 168.

4. Douglas T. Miller, *Henry David Thoreau: A Man for All Seasons* (New York: Facts on File, 1991), p. 104.

5. Henry Beetle Hough, *Thoreau of Walden* (New York: Simon & Schuster, 1956), p. 266.

# GLOSSARY

abolitionist—One who worked to have slavery made illegal.

American Civil War—War between the North and South from 1861 to 1865 over slavery and other issues.

depression—A period of low business activity and widespread unemployment.

Fugitive Slave Law—A law making it mandatory to return a runaway slave to his or her master.

graphite—A powdery black substance used to make pencil lead.

house-raising—A gathering of neighbors to help build a house.

Lyceum—An organization in Concord that promoted lectures.

Penobscot—An American Indian tribe in Maine.

phrenology—A practice of analyzing one's character by studying the shape of his or her skull. This theory has been proven inaccurate.

poll tax—A tax on individuals rather than on property where each person is taxed the same, whether they are rich or poor.

scarlet fever—A contagious disease whose symptoms are a sore throat, fever, and a red rash.

surveying—The science of determining land boundaries by measuring.

tetanus—An infectious disease that usually enters the body through an open wound.

transcendentalism—A philosophy based on the belief that knowledge of all things, including God, does not only come from experience and observation. Transcendentalists believed that each person must use reasoning to determine the true nature of God and the world.

tuberculosis—An infectious disease of the lungs.

Unitarian—A Christian church that believes in moral teachings but not in the Trinity, made up of God, Jesus, and the Holy Spirit.

Utopian—Idealistic.

# FURTHER READING

Anderson, Peter. *Henry David Thoreau: American Naturalist*. Danbury, Conn.: Franklin Watts, Inc., 1995.

Crocitto, Frank, ed. *New Suns Will Arise: From the Journal of Henry David Thoreau*. New York: Hyperion Books for Children, 2000.

Miller, Douglas T. *Henry David Thoreau: A Man for All Seasons*. Bridgewater, N.J.: Replica Books, 1999.

Reef, Catherine. *Henry David Thoreau: A Neighbor to Nature*. Brookfield, Conn.: Twenty-first Century Books, 1995.

# INTERNET ADDRESSES

Lenat, Lewis. *Henry David Thoreau*. September 16, 2002. <http://eserver.org/thoreau/thoreau.html>.

Lewis, Jone Johnson. *Henry David Thoreau (1817–1862): A Guide to Resources on Henry David Thoreau*. © 1995–2002. <http://www.transcendentalists.com/1thorea.html>.

The Thoreau Institute at Walden Woods. *The Henry D. Thoreau Home Page*. © 2001. <http://www.walden.org/thoreau/>.

# INDEX